THE INTELLIGENT SPECULATOR

A Unique Approach to Trading Commodities

THE INTELLIGENT SPECULATOR

A Unique Approach to Trading Commodities

RALPH J. FESSENDEN

with JOHN D. McDIVITT

IRWIN
Professional Publishing®
Chicago • London • Singapore

▼▼ Times Mirror
Ⓜ Higher Education Group

Library of Congress Cataloging-in-Publication Data

Fessenden, Ralph J., 1932–
  The intelligent speculator : a unique approach to trading
commodities / Ralph J. Fessenden with John D. McDivitt.
    p. cm.
  Includes index.
  ISBN 0-7863-0839-7
  1. Commodity exchanges. 2. Speculation. I. McDivitt, John D.
II. Title.
HG6046.F47 1996
332. 63′28—dc20   96–4731

Printed in the United States of America
1 2 3 4 5 6 7 8 9 0 BS 3 2 1 0 9 8 7 6

If you are a speculator, then this book is for you. It describes a unique system of commodity speculation, called *Interval Trading,* a blend of the two well-known speculation methods—trend following and oscillation techniques.

The book begins with a description of speculation and, in particular, commodity speculation. Chapter 2 contains a discussion of the mechanics of commodity trading for those with little or no experience in the field. The description of Interval Trading, itself, begins with Chapter 3. Topics such as the upper-trading level, the interval size, drawdown, and rollovers are covered in subsequent chapters. Like all trading methods, Interval Trading is not infallible. In Chapter 8 we attempt to alert you to "What Can Go Wrong" and what to do about it. Examples of Interval Trading, along with tables, daily charts, and summaries of recent markets are given in Chapter 10.

The authors wish to gratefully acknowledge *Investor's Business Daily* for the wheat quotes used in Chapter 2.

CONTENTS

Chapter 4

Drawdown   53

Chapter 5

The Principal Variables in Interval Trading   63

Chapter 6

Rollovers   83

Chapter 7

The Sell-Buy: More Profits at Lower Risk   95

CHAPTER 1

Speculating in Commodities

Speculation ranks among the most exciting of all human activities. You pit your wits against the market, that malevolent, money-eating monster that lurks in all quote machines. Few human emotions surpass the feeling you get when you win. You beat the market! For most speculators, it is a rare feeling.

Speculation is not gambling. In gambling, you bet your money and hope for the best. You know the odds are against you but you believe your luck will beat the odds. Intellect is not needed, just good luck. Without knowledge, trading commodities is just gambling. The odds will be against you and, chances are, you will lose. With knowledge, however, the odds in commodity trading shift in your favor. You are no longer gambling. You are using your wits to try to beat the market. You are speculating.

If you are a speculator, then this book is for you. It describes a successful and conservative speculation method called Interval Trading.

Chapter 2 is for the beginning speculator. It contains a brief discussion of the mechanics of futures (commodity) trading, commodity price movement, and how commodity prices are forecasted. However, no attempt is made to cover all the topics a beginning speculator must master to successfully trade commodities. If you are a beginner, consider Chapter 2 to be a brief introduction to the subject. If you are an experienced commodity trader, skip Chapter 2 and start with Chapter 3.

Chapter 3 introduces the basic principles of Interval Trading. Chapter 7 completes the discussion by introducing a new concept—the buy-sell—a technique that allows Interval Trading to bridge the gap between oscillatory and trend-following methods. The chapters between these two—Chapters 4, 5 and 6—discuss the principal features of Interval Trading. These subjects include drawdown and the amount of capital you will need, how the amount of capital you will need depends upon the interval, and what to do when the contract approaches expiration. Chapter 8 discusses the conditions under which Interval Trading fails. The remaining portions of the book are devoted to examples and miscellaneous topics for a beginning speculator.

A. RISK AND SPECULATION

Investments vary dramatically in their risk. At one extreme are the very safe, very conservative investments, such as CDs and T-bills. These investments are interest-bearing and the monies that will accrue can be calculated at the time of purchase. At the opposite end of the investment spectrum are speculative, high-risk investments, such as futures trading. Large sums of money can be made trading futures. However, if you are not very careful, large sums can also be lost.

Risk in highly speculative stocks and futures depends, in part, on your attitude. Speculative attitude can be likened to a spectrum. At one extreme is the attitude held by the aggressive speculator. This individual is out to make a killing. His or her goal is to pyramid $10,000 into $1,000,000 in as short a time as possible. Winning for this individual is of the utmost importance. Everything is on the line all of the time.

Certainly, it is possible to pyramid $10,000 into $1,000,000, but to do so is more akin to gambling than investing. You could also make a million by "investing" in lottery tickets. However, the chance of making a million by either method is rather remote. Most likely you will just lose your money.

At the other end of the speculation spectrum is the attitude of the conservative speculator. The goal of this individual is to obtain a high rate of return on his or her capital and not lose capital in the process.

B. TRADING SYSTEMS

There are two major groups of commodity trading systems in use today—oscillatory systems and trend-following systems. Both of these trading techniques are very powerful (lucrative) under proper market conditions. Oscillatory systems work best in a sideways market but fail when the market starts to trend. Trend-following methods work best when the market is trending but fail when the market moves sideways. Thus, these systems are complementary. It would seem that all a speculator would have to do to make money is to determine which type of system should be used at what point in time. This turns out to be extremely difficult to do.

This book presents another technique for commodity speculation, called Interval Trading. When you Interval Trade, you will not pyramid $10,000 into $1,000,000. But with skill and understanding, you should be able to make a yearly return of 20 to 50 percent. Thus, Interval Trading is a conservative method of speculation suitable for the intelligent speculator.

Interval Trading tries to circumvent the problem of system choice by being at once an oscillatory and a trend-following technique. Unfortunately, like all other trading systems, Interval Trading has its strengths and weaknesses. Interval Trading works best when trading starts near a major bottom in a sideways market that turns and trends up. Interval Trading does poorly when trading starts near a major top in a market that turns and trends down.

Interval Trading requires some skill at fundamental and technical analysis of the markets. This book does not deal with these subjects nor their application to Interval Trading. Rather, this book is limited to a discussion of the principles of Interval Trading and examples of its applications.

C. COMMODITIES TO TRADE

In Interval Trading, we limit our trades to the metals, the energy futures (crude oil and derivatives), and the agricultural commodities. We do not trade the financial instruments (interest rate futures, the stock indexes, and the currencies). Therefore, we will refer to our activity as commodity trading. The principal commodities we recommend for Interval Trading are listed in Table 1–1 along with the exchange at which they are traded.

D. INTERVAL TRADING VERSUS SCALE TRADING

Interval Trading is a variation of the Scale-Trading technique described by Robert F. Wiest in his book *You Can't Lose Trading Commodities* (Robert F. Wiest, PO Box 3882, Westlake Village, CA 91359). Although his title is an exaggeration, the concept is brilliant and, like many brilliant ideas, extremely simple. This book describes both the basic concept of Scale Trading and our variations and improvements that we believe decrease risk and enhance profitability. We call our variation *Interval Trading* to differentiate it from Wiest's *Scale Trading*.

For those of you familiar with Scale Trading, the principal differences between Scale Trading and Interval Trading are as follows:

1. In Interval Trading, no attempt is made to predict a bottom. Trading is continuous regardless of the price drop. In Scale Trading, a price bottom is predicted and trading continues down to that level but not below it.

2. In Interval Trading, trading continues as long as the price remains below the upper trading level. In Scale Trading, there is no provision to trade above the price of the first long purchase.

3. In Interval Trading, large price differences between purchases are used and oscillation profits (see Chapter 3) are captured by using a sell-buy strategy. In Scale Trading, oscillation profits are captured by using a small price difference between purchases.

Because of these differences, a quantitative comparison of the two trading methods cannot be made.

TABLE 1-1

Commodities Recommended for Interval Trading

Commodity	Exchange
Grains and Oilseeds	
Corn	CBOT
Oats	CBOT
Soybeans	CBOT
Soybean meal	CBOT
Soybean oil	CBOT
Wheat, soft red winter	CBOT
Wheat, hard red winter	KC
Wheat, spring	MPLS
Food and Fibers	
Cocoa	CSCE
Coffee	CSCE
Cotton	NYCE
Orange juice, frozen	NYCE
Sugar #11 (World)	CSCE
Lumber, random lengths	CME
Energy Complex	
Crude oil	NYMEX
Heating oil	NYMEX
Unleaded gasoline	NYMEX
Natural gas	NYMEX
Livestock and Meat	
Feeder cattle	CME
Live cattle	CME
Live hogs	CME
Pork bellies	CME
Metals	
Copper (high grade)	COMEX
Gold	COMEX
Palladium	NYMEX
Platinum	NYMEX
Silver (5,000 oz)	COMEX

CBOT — Chicago Board of Trade
CME — Chicago Mercantile Exchange
COMEX — (CMA, Div. NYM) Commodity Exchange, New York (COMEX Division of New York Merchantile Exchange)
CSCE — Coffee, Sugar and Cocoa Exchange
KC — Kansas City Board of Trade
MPLS — Minneapolis Grain Exchange
NYCE — New York Cotton Exchange

E. A CAVEAT

Before we begin, a caveat is in order. Conservative speculation is still speculation. No matter how it is titled, speculation carries with it a high risk of capital loss. Speculation and high risk go hand in hand. Commodity price movements can be drastic and unexpected. Consequently, you should never risk more than you can afford to lose. To do so courts financial disaster.

The Mechanics of Commodity Speculation

This chapter is for the beginning trader who wishes to become familiar with the field of commodity speculation. If you are an old hand at the commodity game, skip this chapter because it contains nothing you don't already know. However, if you have traded stocks and find that to be an exciting activity but know very little about commodities, then read on. This chapter provides you with what you need to know to understand Interval Trading. However, this chapter will not provide you everything you need to know to successfully trade commodities. It is merely an introduction to the field.

A. THE CONTRACT MARKETS

Futures trading involves the purchase and sale of contracts to deliver a financial instrument or commodity at a specific date in the future. Commodity trading generally refers to that portion of futures trading that deals with a physical article, such as wheat, silver, or crude oil. We will emphasize commodity trading because that is our vehicle for Interval Trading.

When you purchase a commodity futures contract, you purchase a contract to accept delivery of that commodity at a specific date in the future. For example, if you purchase a contract of December wheat, you have purchased the obligation to accept delivery of, and pay for, 5,000 bushels of wheat next December.

Chances are excellent you do not want 5,000 bushels of wheat. Therefore, you will sell your contract some time between the time you purchased it and next December. This second transaction is called the *offset* or *offsetting sale*. If the price of wheat goes up while you owned the December wheat contract, then you can sell the contract for more than you paid for it and, consequently, make money. Of course, if the price goes down, you will have to sell it for less than you paid for it and you will lose money.

Commodity futures contracts that are traded on an exchange are standardized in all respects except for price. For example, the grade, or type, of wheat that can be delivered to fulfill a Chicago Board of Trade contract is restricted to soft red wheat. Hard wheats are traded on the Kansas City Board of Trade and the Minneapolis Grain Exchange.

While the grade of a commodity is standardized, its price is not. It is left open and determined at the time of purchase. When you tell your broker to buy a December wheat contract (5,000 bushels), your order is relayed through the broker's commission house to their floor broker at the exchange. Your order is executed by an open outcry by that floor broker in the Wheat Pit, a specific location on the floor of the exchange where wheat contracts are traded. The result of the transaction (its purchase price) is routed back through the commission house to your broker who, in turn, calls you. The time between entering your order with the broker and its actual execution on the floor of the exchange is a matter of minutes. (There is, of course, a lot of paperwork generated by your transaction. You and your broker will receive some of this paper, but a lot of it will remain invisible to you.)

B. YOUR ACCOUNT AND MARGIN

When you open an account with a commodity broker, you will be asked, among other things, for a deposit. The money you deposit must be held by an authorized brokerage firm (called a commission house or futures commission merchant [FCM]) and not by the broker. You will receive a monthly accounting from the brokerage firm as well as interim reports as you buy and sell contracts.

Your deposit is not margin. Margin is the deposit required by the exchange when a commodity futures contract is bought or sold. The broker's commission house makes this deposit for you. They in turn want your money in an account with them before they do business for you.

C. COMMODITY FUTURES ARE HIGHLY LEVERAGED INVESTMENTS

Before you can buy a commodity futures contract, you must have sufficient funds deposited with the brokerage firm to cover the margin. Let's calculate what percent this margin is of the contract's total value. Suppose you purchase a contract of December wheat for $3.00 a bushel. A wheat contract contains 5,000 bushels. Consequently, the value of contract is:

$$5,000 \text{ bushels} \times \$3.00 \text{ per bushel} = \$15,000$$

What you have purchased is the contractual right to receive 5,000 bushels of wheat next December and the obligation to remit $15,000 at the time you receive that wheat. For this privilege, the brokerage firm debits your existing account by the amount of the margin.

Margin for wheat is about $675. This value is determined by the exchange and the brokerage firm and not by the broker you deal with. (We will discuss margin in more detail later.) Therefore, the margin is

$$(\$675/\$15,000) \times 100 = 4.5\%$$

of the total value of the contract. For $675 you "own" a contract worth $15,000. Commodities are highly leveraged. It is this leverage that makes trading commodity futures so lucrative when you are right and so disastrous when you are wrong. If the price of December wheat increases by five cents (from $3.00 to $3.05), then the value of your contract increases from $15,000 to $15,250. If you sell your contract at $3.05, your profit would be $250, a $(250/675) \times 100$ or 37 percent return on the money needed for margin.

Commodity futures trading is highly speculative. You can make gigantic amounts of money or lose vast fortunes rapidly. This speculative value is not due to the huge price swings of the commodities themselves, but to their enormous leverage.

From a practical standpoint, your deposit with the brokerage firm is to protect the brokerage firm against your default on the contract. The brokerage firm is a profit-making institution. They are required by the exchange to deposit their own money as margin for the contracts they purchase for you. In addition, they are required to make good on your default should it occur. To protect themselves, the brokerage firm requires you to maintain ample funds in your account to cover your obligations. Should the market turn against you, the value of your account will decrease accordingly. At some point, the brokerage firm will issue a margin call, a request for additional funds. If you fail to meet the margin call (add money to your account), your broker will liquidate your contracts so that a positive balance can be maintained. When you open your account, you give them permission to do this should the need arise.

D. WHERE TO GET COMMODITY PRICES

Timely information is imperative for successful commodity trading. Where to get this information and what it means often stumps the beginning commodity trader. There are actually a number of different sources for current information.

Your Broker

For up-to-the-minute quotes, call your broker. He or she can give you the last quote from the quote machine. Don't make a pest of yourself. They will be glad to talk to you but don't wear out your welcome.

Computer Services

You can subscribe to any of several data services that provide quotes. These services are very convenient and inexpensive. To find vendors for these services, buy a copy of *Futures* or *Technical Analysis of Stocks and Commodities* from your local magazine store and look for their advertisements.

In general, you can purchase three different types of quotes. *Up-to-the-minute* quotes (called tick-by-tick quotes) are the most expensive and usually not needed unless you are a day trader. *Delayed* quotes cost less. They are about 10 to 30 minutes behind the market. *End-of-day* quotes are the least expensive.

FIGURE 2-1

Wheat Quotations for 10/4/95, as Found in the *Investor's Business Daily* on 10/5/95.

Wheat (CBOT)—5,000 bu minimum—dollars per bushel
Est. Vol. 14,000 Vol. 11,156 open int 100,475 + 9,400

4.96 3/4	3.42	Dec	64,947	4.84 1/2	4.86	4.81 1/2	4.85 1/2	−.01
5.03	3.46	Mar	23,921	4.94 1/2	4.95	4.90 1/2	4.94 1/2	−.00 1/2
4.66	3.79	May	2,770	4.59	4.59 1/2	4.57	4.59	−.02
4.18	3.25	Jul	8,487	4.10	4.12 1/2	4.09	4.11 3/4	——
4.20	3.74	Sep	148	4.14	4.14 1/2	4.12	4.14 1/2	−.01
4.30	3.62	Dec	202	4.25	4.26	4.22	4.26	−.00 1/2

Wheat (KBOT)—5,000 bu minimum—dollars per bushel
Vol. 3,477 open int 39,075 − 480

5.03 1/2	3.43	Dec	23,918	4.96	4.99 3/4	4.94 1/4	4.99 1/2	+.02
5.02	3.44 1/2	Mar	12,015	4.95 1/2	4.98	4.93	4.98	+.01 1/2
4.73	3.68	May	806	4.65	4.68 1/2	4.65	4.68 1/2	+.01 1/2
4.30	3.30	Jul	2,170	4.21	4.23 1/4	4.20	4.23	+.01
4.31 1/2	3.87	Sep	165	4.25	4.26 1/2	4.25	4.26	+.00 1/2

Wheat (MPLS)—5,000 bu minimum—dollars per bushel
Vol. 2,730 open int 20,138 − 409

4.97	3.43 1/2	Dec	15,230	4.87 1/2	4.93	4.86 1/2	4.92 1/4	+.03
5.05	3.58	Mar	4,265	4.97	4.98 1/2	4.94 3/4	4.97 1/2	−.00 1/4
4.96	3.46	May	418	4.89	4.89	4.85 1/2	4.88	−.01 3/4
4.64 1/2	3.79	Jul	196	4.57 1/2	4.58 1/2	4.56 1/2	4.58 1/2	−.01 1/2
4.63	3.95	Sep	24	4.28	4.30	4.27	4.30	+.03
4.32	4.20	Dec	4				4.35	+.03

Reprinted with permission from *Investor's Business Daily,* 5 October 1995, B8.

Newspapers

Many local newspapers carry limited amounts of commodity quotations. Nationally distributed financial newspapers, such as the *Investor's Business Daily,* carry nearly complete listings of daily commodity prices.

E. HOW TO READ PRICE QUOTATIONS

Figure 2–1 shows quotations for three different grades of wheat traded on different exchanges taken from the 10/5/95 *Investor's Business Daily.* Since all quotations are similar to these quotes, we will use them to explain the symbolism.

FIGURE 2-2

The Exchange Designation

The Exchange designation

Wheat (CBOT) —5,000 bu minimum—dollars per bushel

Est. Vol. 14,000 Vol. 11,156 open int 100,475 + 9,400

4.96 3/4	3.42	Dec	64,947	4.84 1/2	4.86	4.81 1/2	4.85 1/2	−.01
5.03	3.46	Mar	23,921	4.94 1/2	4.95	4.90 1/2	4.94 1/2	−.00 1/2
4.66	3.79	May	2,770	4.59	4.59 1/2	4.57	4.59	−.02
4.18	3.25	Jul	8,487	4.10	4.12 1/2	4.09	4.11 3/4	——
4.20	3.74	Sep	148	4.14	4.14 1/2	4.12	4.14 1/2	−.01
4.30	3.62	Dec	202	4.25	4.26	4.22	4.26	−.00 1/2

Wheat (KBOT)—5,000 bu minimum—dollars per bushel
Vol. 3,477 open int 39,075 − 480

5.03 1/2	3.43	Dec	23,918	4.96	4.99 3/4	4.94 1/4	4.99 1/2	+.02
5.02	3.44 1/2	Mar	12,015	4.95 1/2	4.98	4.93	4.98	+.01 1/2
4.73	3.68	May	806	4.65	4.68 1/2	4.65	4.68 1/2	+.01 1/2
4.30	3.30	Jul	2,170	4.21	4.23 1/4	4.20	4.23	+.01
4.31 1/2	3.87	Sep	165	4.25	4.26 1/2	4.25	4.26	+.00 1/2

Wheat (MPLS)—5,000 bu minimum—dollars per bushel
Vol. 2,730 open int 20,138 − 409

4.97	3.43 1/2	Dec	15,230	4.87 1/2	4.93	4.86 1/2	4.92 1/4	+.03
5.05	3.58	Mar	4,265	4.97	4.98 1/2	4.94 3/4	4.97 1/2	−.00 1/4
4.96	3.46	May	418	4.89	4.89	4.85 1/2	4.88	−.01 3/4
4.64 1/2	3.79	Jul	196	4.57 1/2	4.58 1/2	4.56 1/2	4.58 1/2	−.01 1/2
4.63	3.95	Sep	24	4.28	4.30	4.27	4.30	+.03
4.32	4.20	Dec	4				4.35	+.03

Reprinted with permission from *Investor's Business Daily*, 5 October 1995, B8.

Wheat is traded on three domestic exchanges: the Chicago Board of Trade (CBOT or CBT), the Kansas City Board of Trade (KBOT or KC), and the Minneapolis Grain Exchange (MPLS). The grade of wheat traded on each of these exchanges is different, and, consequently, the wheat contracts are not interchangeable. The exchange is listed in the first line immediately following the word "Wheat" (see Figure 2–2).

FIGURE 2-3

The Contract and Its Opening Price

December CBOT wheat opened trading at 4.84 1/2 ($4.845) a bushel on 10/4/95

Wheat (CBOT)—5,000 bu minimum—dollars per bushel
Est. Vol. 14,000 Vol. 11,156 open int 100,475 + 9,400

4.96 3/4	3.42	Dec	64,947	4.84 1/2	4.86	4.81 1/2	4.85 1/2	−.01
5.03	3.46	Mar	23,921	4.94 1/2	4.95	4.90 1/2	4.94 1/2	−.00 1/2
4.66	3.79	May	2,770	4.59	4.59 1/2	4.57	4.59	−.02
4.18	3.25	Jul	8,487	4.10	4.12 1/2	4.09	4.11 3/4	——
4.20	3.74	Sep	148	4.14	4.14 1/2	4.12	4.14 1/2	−.01
4.30	3.62	Dec	202	4.25	4.26	4.22	4.26	−.00 1/2

Wheat (KBOT)—5,000 bu minimum—dollars per bushel
Vol. 3,477 open int 39,075 − 480

5.03 1/2	3.43	Dec	23,918	4.96	4.99 3/4	4.94 1/4	4.99 1/2	+.02
5.02	3.44 1/2	Mar	12,015	4.95 1/2	4.98	4.93	4.98	+.01 1/2
4.73	3.68	May	806	4.65	4.68 1/2	4.65	4.68 1/2	+.01 1/2
4.30	3.30	Jul	2,170	4.21	4.23 1/4	4.20	4.23	+.01
4.31 1/2	3.87	Sep	165	4.25	4.26 1/2	4.25	4.26	+.00 1/2

Wheat (MPLS)—5,000 bu minimum—dollars per bushel
Vol. 2,730 open int 20,138 − 409

4.97	3.43 1/2	Dec	15,230	4.87 1/2	4.93	4.86 1/2	4.92 1/4	+.03
5.05	3.58	Mar	4,265	4.97	4.98 1/2	4.94 3/4	4.97 1/2	−.00 1/4
4.96	3.46	May	418	4.89	4.89	4.85 1/2	4.88	−.01 3/4
4.64 1/2	3.79	Jul	196	4.57 1/2	4.58 1/2	4.56 1/2	4.58 1/2	−.01 1/2
4.63	3.95	Sep	24	4.28	4.30	4.27	4.30	+.03
4.32	4.20	Dec	4				4.35	+.03

Reprinted with permission from *Investor's Business Daily,* 5 October 1995, B8.

Following the exchange designation, the size of the contract is listed. It is the same for all three exchanges: 5,000 bushels (bu). The last item on the header line is the monetary units for the quote, which for wheat is dollars per bushel.

The expiration month for the contract is listed toward the left followed by the opening price for the day. The opening price on 10/4/95 for the CBOT 1995 December contract was 4.84 1/2 ($4.845) per bushel (see Figure 2–3).

FIGURE 2-4

The Trading Range and Close

The trading range for December wheat was 4.86–4.815

The close was 4.855

Wheat (CBOT)—5,000 bu minimum—dollars per bushel
Est. Vol. 14,000 Vol. 11,156 open int 100,475 + 9,400

4.96 3/4	3.42	Dec	64,947	4.84 1/2	(4.86)	4.81 1/2	(4.85 1/2)	–.01
5.03	3.46	Mar	23,921	4.94 1/2	4.95	4.90 1/2	4.94 1/2	–.00 1/2
4.66	3.79	May	2,770	4.59	4.59 1/2	4.57	4.59	–.02
4.18	3.25	Jul	8,487	4.10	4.12 1/2	4.09	4.11 3/4	——
4.20	3.74	Sep	148	4.14	4.14 1/2	4.12	4.14 1/2	–.01
4.30	3.62	Dec	202	4.25	4.26	4.22	4.26	–.00 1/2

Wheat (KBOT)—5,000 bu minimum—dollars per bushel
Vol. 3,477 open int 39,075 – 480

5.03 1/2	3.43	Dec	23,918	4.96	4.99 3/4	4.94 1/4	4.99 1/2	+.02
5.02	3.44 1/2	Mar	12,015	4.95 1/2	4.98	4.93	4.98	+.01 1/2
4.73	3.68	May	806	4.65	4.68 1/2	4.65	4.68 1/2	+.01 1/2
4.30	3.30	Jul	2,170	4.21	4.23 1/4	4.20	4.23	+.01
4.31 1/2	3.87	Sep	165	4.25	4.26 1/2	4.25	4.26	+.00 1/2

Wheat (MPLS)—5,000 bu minimum—dollars per bushel
Vol. 2,730 open int 20,138 – 409

4.97	3.43 1/2	Dec	15,230	4.87 1/2	4.93	4.86 1/2	4.92 1/4	+.03
5.05	3.58	Mar	4,265	4.97	4.98 1/2	4.94 3/4	4.97 1/2	–.00 1/4
4.96	3.46	May	418	4.89	4.89	4.85 1/2	4.88	–.01 3/4
4.64 1/2	3.79	Jul	196	4.57 1/2	4.58 1/2	4.56 1/2	4.58 1/2	–.01 1/2
4.63	3.95	Sep	24	4.28	4.30	4.27	4.30	+.03
4.32	4.20	Dec	4				4.35	+.03

Reprinted with permission from *Investor's Business Daily,* 5 October 1995, B8.

Following the opening price on the same line is the high and then the low price for that trading day. The high is the highest price paid for a bushel of wheat during the trading day and the low is the lowest price paid. There is no indication of which came first. To find this out, you would need the time sequence of quotes as they occurred during the day, called tick-by-tick quotes. Such data is available, but voluminous and costly.

The daily price range, or just the range, for the CBOT 1995 December contract on 10/4/95 was 4.86–4.81 1/2 (see Figure 2–4). December wheat traded within a 4 1/2 cents range.

TABLE 2-1

Quote Machine Eighths Equivalents

Last Digit in Quote	Eighths Equivalent
0	0/8 or 0
1	1/8
2	2/8 or 1/4
3	3/8
4	4/8 or 1/2
5	5/8
6	6/8 or 3/4
7	7/8

The next price on the line, 4.85 1/2 (see Figure 2–4), is the official closing price for 10/4/95. During the final minutes of trading, called the "close," several transactions are completed at slightly different prices. A representative price is selected from this group and designated as the settlement price, the official close. For simplicity, the settlement price is often just called the close.

Note that the open, low, and close are quoted with a fraction. The grain futures are traded in quarters (1/4) of a cent. Glancing at the other quotes in the figure you can see many fractions. With a computer, fractions are extremely difficult to store, transmit, and display. Therefore, a different notation is used. On a computer screen, the settlement price (4.85 1/2) would have been displayed as 4854, where the terminal (least significant digit) "4" means 4/8 (or 1/2).

Quote machines must be able to reflect eighths as well as quarters because options are traded in eighths. Therefore, an eighths notation that accommodates both types of quotations is used. The quote machine notations for eighths is listed in Table 2–1.

Returning to the explanation of newspaper price quotations, a −.01 is displayed in Figure 2–5 just after the settlement price. This value is the difference between this day's (10/4/95) settlement price and that of the previous day (10/3/95). With a change of −.01, the previous day's settlement price must have been 4.86 1/2. Your broker would have said "December wheat was down 1 today" to convey the same information.

FIGURE 2-5

Comparison of Settlement Prices

December wheat was down 1 point ($0.01) from yesterday's
settlement price. a bushel

Wheat (CBOT)—5,000 bu minimum—dollars per bushel
Est. Vol. 14,000 Vol. 11,156 open int 100,475 + 9,400

4.96 3/4	3.42	Dec	64,947	4.84 1/2	4.86	4.81 1/2	4.85 1/2	−.01
5.03	3.46	Mar	23,921	4.94 1/2	4.95	4.90 1/2	4.94 1/2	−.00 1/2
4.66	3.79	May	2,770	4.59	4.59 1/2	4.57	4.59	−.02
4.18	3.25	Jul	8,487	4.10	4.12 1/2	4.09	4.11 3/4	——
4.20	3.74	Sep	148	4.14	4.14 1/2	4.12	4.14 1/2	−.01
4.30	3.62	Dec	202	4.25	4.26	4.22	4.26	−.00 1/2

Wheat (KBOT)—5,000 bu minimum—dollars per bushel
Vol. 3,477 open int 39,075 − 480

5.03 1/2	3.43	Dec	23,918	4.96	4.99 3/4	4.94 1/4	4.99 1/2	+.02
5.02	3.44 1/2	Mar	12,015	4.95 1/2	4.98	4.93	4.98	+.01 1/2
4.73	3.68	May	806	4.65	4.68 1/2	4.65	4.68 1/2	+.01 1/2
4.30	3.30	Jul	2,170	4.21	4.23 1/4	4.20	4.23	+.01
4.31 1/2	3.87	Sep	165	4.25	4.26 1/2	4.25	4.26	+.00 1/2

Wheat (MPLS)—5,000 bu minimum—dollars per bushel
Vol. 2,730 open int 20,138 − 409

4.97	3.43 1/2	Dec	15,230	4.87 1/2	4.93	4.86 1/2	4.92 1/4	+.03
5.05	3.58	Mar	4,265	4.97	4.98 1/2	4.94 3/4	4.97 1/2	−.00 1/4
4.96	3.46	May	418	4.89	4.89	4.85 1/2	4.88	−.01 3/4
4.64 1/2	3.79	Jul	196	4.57 1/2	4.58 1/2	4.56 1/2	4.58 1/2	−.01 1/2
4.63	3.95	Sep	24	4.28	4.30	4.27	4.30	+.03
4.32	4.20	Dec	4				4.35	+.03

Reprinted with permission from *Investor's Business Daily,* 5 October 1995, B8.

The next two prices (4.96 3/4 and 3.42) are the highest and lowest price paid during the lifetime of the 1995 December contract. These two prices make up the price range for the life of the 1995 December contract as of 10/4/95 (see Figure 2–6).

Just after "Dec" on the line is the open interest (64,947) for the December contract (see Figure 2–7). Open interest is the number of open contracts. It is the commodity's equivalent of the number of outstanding shares of a stock issued by a corporation.

F I G U R E 2-6

The Contract's High and Low Price

December contract high and low

Wheat (CBOT)—5,000 bu minimum—dollars per bushel
Est. Vol. 14,000 Vol. 11,156 open int 100,475 + 9,400

4.96 3/4	3.42	Dec	64,947	4.84 1/2	4.86	4.81 1/2	4.85 1/2	−.01
5.03	3.46	Mar	23,921	4.94 1/2	4.95	4.90 1/2	4.94 1/2	−.00 1/2
4.66	3.79	May	2,770	4.59	4.59 1/2	4.57	4.59	−.02
4.18	3.25	Jul	8,487	4.10	4.12 1/2	4.09	4.11 3/4	——
4.20	3.74	Sep	148	4.14	4.14 1/2	4.12	4.14 1/2	−.01
4.30	3.62	Dec	202	4.25	4.26	4.22	4.26	−.00 1/2

Wheat (KBOT)—5,000 bu minimum—dollars per bushel
Vol. 3,477 open int 39,075 − 480

5.03 1/2	3.43	Dec	23,918	4.96	4.99 3/4	4.94 1/4	4.99 1/2	+.02
5.02	3.44 1/2	Mar	12,015	4.95 1/2	4.98	4.93	4.98	+.01 1/2
4.73	3.68	May	806	4.65	4.68 1/2	4.65	4.68 1/2	+.01 1/2
4.30	3.30	Jul	2,170	4.21	4.23 1/4	4.20	4.23	+.01
4.31 1/2	3.87	Sep	165	4.25	4.26 1/2	4.25	4.26	+.00 1/2

Wheat (MPLS)—5,000 bu minimum—dollars per bushel
Vol. 2,730 open int 20,138 − 409

4.97	3.43 1/2	Dec	15,230	4.87 1/2	4.93	4.86 1/2	4.92 1/4	+.03
5.05	3.58	Mar	4,265	4.97	4.98 1/2	4.94 3/4	4.97 1/2	−.00 1/4
4.96	3.46	May	418	4.89	4.89	4.85 1/2	4.88	−.01 3/4
4.64 1/2	3.79	Jul	196	4.57 1/2	4.58 1/2	4.56 1/2	4.58 1/2	−.01 1/2
4.63	3.95	Sep	24	4.28	4.30	4.27	4.30	+.03
4.32	4.20	Dec	4				4.35	+.03

Reprinted with permission from *Investor's Business Daily,* 5 October 1995, B8.

Open interest gives us an idea of the liquidity of the market. If open interest for the contract is small, few people hold contracts and you may have trouble getting your orders filled at the time you want them filled. Use the open interest of a contract to determine if you should trade that contract month.

For example, if you wanted to buy a KBOT wheat contract for delivery next spring or summer, avoid the May contract because of

FIGURE 2-7

The Open Interest

December open interest

Wheat (CBOT)—5,000 bu minimum—dollars per bushel
Est. Vol. 14,000 Vol. 11,156 open int 100,475 + 9,400

4.96 3/4	3.42	Dec	64,947	4.84 1/2	4.86	4.81 1/2	4.85 1/2	−.01
5.03	3.46	Mar	23,921	4.94 1/2	4.95	4.90 1/2	4.94 1/2	−.00 1/2
4.66	3.79	May	2,770	4.59	4.59 1/2	4.57	4.59	−.02
4.18	3.25	Jul	8,487	4.10	4.12 1/2	4.09	4.11 3/4	——
4.20	3.74	Sep	148	4.14	4.14 1/2	4.12	4.14 1/2	−.01
4.30	3.62	Dec	202	4.25	4.26	4.22	4.26	−.00 1/2

Wheat (KBOT)—5,000 bu minimum—dollars per bushel
Vol. 3,477 open int 39,075 − 480

5.03 1/2	3.43	Dec	23,918	4.96	4.99 3/4	4.94 1/4	4.99 1/2	+.02
5.02	3.44 1/2	Mar	12,015	4.95 1/2	4.98	4.93	4.98	+.01 1/2
4.73	3.68	May	806	4.65	4.68 1/2	4.65	4.68 1/2	+.01 1/2
4.30	3.30	Jul	2,170	4.21	4.23 1/4	4.20	4.23	+.01
4.31 1/2	3.87	Sep	165	4.25	4.26 1/2	4.25	4.26	+.00 1/2

Wheat (MPLS)—5,000 bu minimum—dollars per bushel
Vol. 2,730 open int 20,138 − 409

4.97	3.43 1/2	Dec	15,230	4.87 1/2	4.93	4.86 1/2	4.92 1/4	+.03
5.05	3.58	Mar	4,265	4.97	4.98 1/2	4.94 3/4	4.97 1/2	−.00 1/4
4.96	3.46	May	418	4.89	4.89	4.85 1/2	4.88	−.01 3/4
4.64 1/2	3.79	Jul	196	4.57 1/2	4.58 1/2	4.56 1/2	4.58 1/2	−.01 1/2
4.63	3.95	Sep	24	4.28	4.30	4.27	4.30	+.03
4.32	4.20	Dec	4				4.35	+.03

Reprinted with permission from *Investor's Business Daily*, 5 October 1995, B8.

its low open interest. Place your order for a March or July contract. Both have a much higher open interest (see Figure 2–8).

The last value we need to consider, the estimated volume, is
found at the top of the quotes. The estimated volume for CBOT
wheat was 14,000 contracts on 10/4/95 (see Figure 2–9). The previous day's volume (Tuesday, 10/3/95) was 11,156 contracts. It
takes a day to get an accurate count of the number of contracts
traded. Therefore, the best information we can get for the current
day (Wednesday, 10/4/95) is an estimated volume.

FIGURE 2-8

Contracts with Low Open Interest

Avoid contracts with low open interest

Wheat (CBOT)—5,000 bu minimum—dollars per bushel
Est. Vol. 14,000 Vol. 11,156 open int 100,475 + 9,400

4.96 3/4	3.42	Dec	64,947	4.84 1/2	4.86	4.81 1/2	4.85 1/2	−.01
5.03	3.46	Mar	23,921	4.94 1/2	4.95	4.90 1/2	4.94 1/2	−.00 1/2
4.66	3.79	May	2,770	4.59	4.59 1/2	4.57	4.59	−.02
4.18	3.25	Jul	8,487	4.10	4.12 1/2	4.09	4.11 3/4	——
4.20	3.74	Sep	148	4.14	4.14 1/2	4.12	4.14 1/2	−.01
4.30	3.62	Dec	202	4.25	4.26	4.22	4.26	−.00 1/2

Wheat (KBOT)—5,000 bu minimum—dollars per bushel
Vol. 3,477 open int 39,075 − 480

5.03 1/2	3.43	Dec	23,918	4.96	4.99 3/4	4.94 1/4	4.99 1/2	+.02
5.02	3.44 1/2	Mar	12,015	4.95 1/2	4.98	4.93	4.98	+.01 1/2
4.73	3.68	May	(806)	4.65	4.68 1/2	4.65	4.68 1/2	+.01 1/2
4.30	3.30	Jul	2,170	4.21	4.23 1/4	4.20	4.23	+.01
4.31 1/2	3.87	Sep	(165)	4.25	4.26 1/2	4.25	4.26	+.00 1/2

Wheat (MPLS)—5,000 bu minimum—dollars per bushel
Vol. 2,730 open int 20,138 − 409

4.97	3.43 1/2	Dec	15,230	4.87 1/2	4.93	4.86 1/2	4.92 1/4	+.03
5.05	3.58	Mar	4,265	4.97	4.98 1/2	4.94 3/4	4.97 1/2	−.00 1/4
4.96	3.46	May	418	4.89	4.89	4.85 1/2	4.88	−.01 3/4
4.64 1/2	3.79	Jul	196	4.57 1/2	4.58 1/2	4.56 1/2	4.58 1/2	−.01 1/2
4.63	3.95	Sep	24	4.28	4.30	4.27	4.30	+.03
4.32	4.20	Dec	4				4.35	+.03

Reprinted with permission from *Investor's Business Daily*, 5 October 1995, B8.

Volume is the number of contracts traded during the day. The value provided in newspapers is the sum of all contract months, not just that for a single contract month, such as December or May. Therefore, the estimated volume gives us an idea of the liquidity of the commodity as a whole, not just one contract of that commodity. The higher the volume, the more liquid the market. Consequently, the higher the volume, the easier we will be able to sell or buy a contract.

F I G U R E 2-9

Estimated Previous Day's Volumes

Estimated volume

Previous day's volume

Wheat (CBOT)—5,000 bu minimum—dollars per bushel
Est. Vol. 14,000 Vol. 11,156 open int 100,475 + 9,400

4.96 3/4	3.42	Dec	64,947	4.84 1/2	4.86	4.81 1/2	4.85 1/2	−.01
5.03	3.46	Mar	23,921	4.94 1/2	4.95	4.90 1/2	4.94 1/2	−.00 1/2
4.66	3.79	May	2,770	4.59	4.59 1/2	4.57	4.59	−.02
4.18	3.25	Jul	8,487	4.10	4.12 1/2	4.09	4.11 3/4	——
4.20	3.74	Sep	148	4.14	4.14 1/2	4.12	4.14 1/2	−.01
4.30	3.62	Dec	202	4.25	4.26	4.22	4.26	−.00 1/2

Wheat (KBOT)—5,000 bu minimum—dollars per bushel
Vol. 3,477 open int 39,075 − 480

5.03 1/2	3.43	Dec	23,918	4.96	4.99 3/4	4.94 1/4	4.99 1/2	+.02
5.02	3.44 1/2	Mar	12,015	4.95 1/2	4.98	4.93	4.98	+.01 1/2
4.73	3.68	May	806	4.65	4.68 1/2	4.65	4.68 1/2	+.01 1/2
4.30	3.30	Jul	2,170	4.21	4.23 1/4	4.20	4.23	+.01
4.31 1/2	3.87	Sep	165	4.25	4.26 1/2	4.25	4.26	+.00 1/2

Wheat (MPLS)—5,000 bu minimum—dollars per bushel
Vol. 2,730 open int 20,138 − 409

4.97	3.43 1/2	Dec	15,230	4.87 1/2	4.93	4.86 1/2	4.92 1/4	+.03
5.05	3.58	Mar	4,265	4.97	4.98 1/2	4.94 3/4	4.97 1/2	−.00 1/4
4.96	3.46	May	418	4.89	4.89	4.85 1/2	4.88	−.01 3/4
4.64 1/2	3.79	Jul	196	4.57 1/2	4.58 1/2	4.56 1/2	4.58 1/2	−.01 1/2
4.63	3.95	Sep	24	4.28	4.30	4.27	4.30	+.03
4.32	4.20	Dec	4				4.35	+.03

Reprinted with permission from *Investor's Business Daily*, 5 October 1995, B8.

As a general rule, the nearby contract months always have higher volume and open interest than do the more distant contract months. However, when choosing a contract month to trade, you should ask your broker for the volume of that specific contract. This information is available on their quote machine and is more useful than the estimated volume figure of the commodity as given in the newspaper.

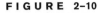

FIGURE 2-10

Component Parts of a Commodity Chart

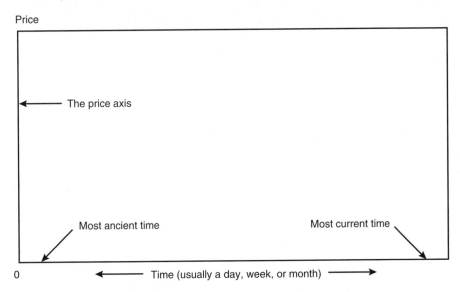

Price

The price axis

Most ancient time   Most current time

0   ⟵——— Time (usually a day, week, or month) ———⟶

F. CHARTS—THE GRAPHICAL PRESENTATION OF COMMODITY PRICES

The graphical presentation of commodity prices is called a chart. The most common type of chart shows price change versus time. Price is plotted on the vertical axis and some unit of time on the horizontal axis (see Figure 2–10).

On the time axis, time increases from left to right. The oldest quotes are plotted to the far left on the chart and the most recent quote is plotted on the farthest right. The most common time units are day, week, and month.

The price data is plotted as a bar. Each bar represents the high-to-low price range for the time period. For example, on a daily chart, the top of the bar is the daily high and the bottom of the bar is the daily low. The opening price is plotted as a tick on the left side of the bar and the close a tick on the right side (see Figure 2–11).

For a weekly chart, the opening price is the price on Monday morning, and the close is the settlement price on Friday. In a

FIGURE 2–11

The Price Bar Used in Commodity Charts

similar vein, on the monthly chart the opening price is the price on the opening of the first day of the month and the closing is the settlement price on the last day of the month.

Typical daily, weekly, and monthly charts are given in Figures 2–12, 2–13, and 2–14. These three charts show the same commodity (wheat) during the same time period, and all three end on the same day.

If more than one contract month is combined for the construction of a chart, (usually found in weekly and monthly charts), there is no transition price to join the two months. One week or month abruptly ends and the other starts. This can result in a discontinuity in the price pattern, which appears as a huge drop or rise in the price of the commodity. See Figure 2–13 for an example of a price discontinuity arising from a change in contract months.

Price discontinuity between contract months arises because of the different values of the commodity during different times of

Daily Chart of 1995 CBOT December Wheat, 1/3/95 to 10/13/95

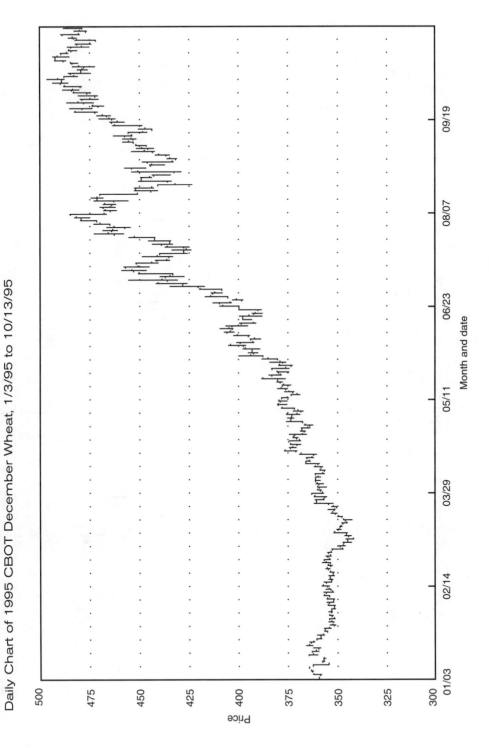

FIGURE 2-13

Weekly Chart of Combined 1994 March and 1995 December CBOT Wheat, 2/94 to 10/95

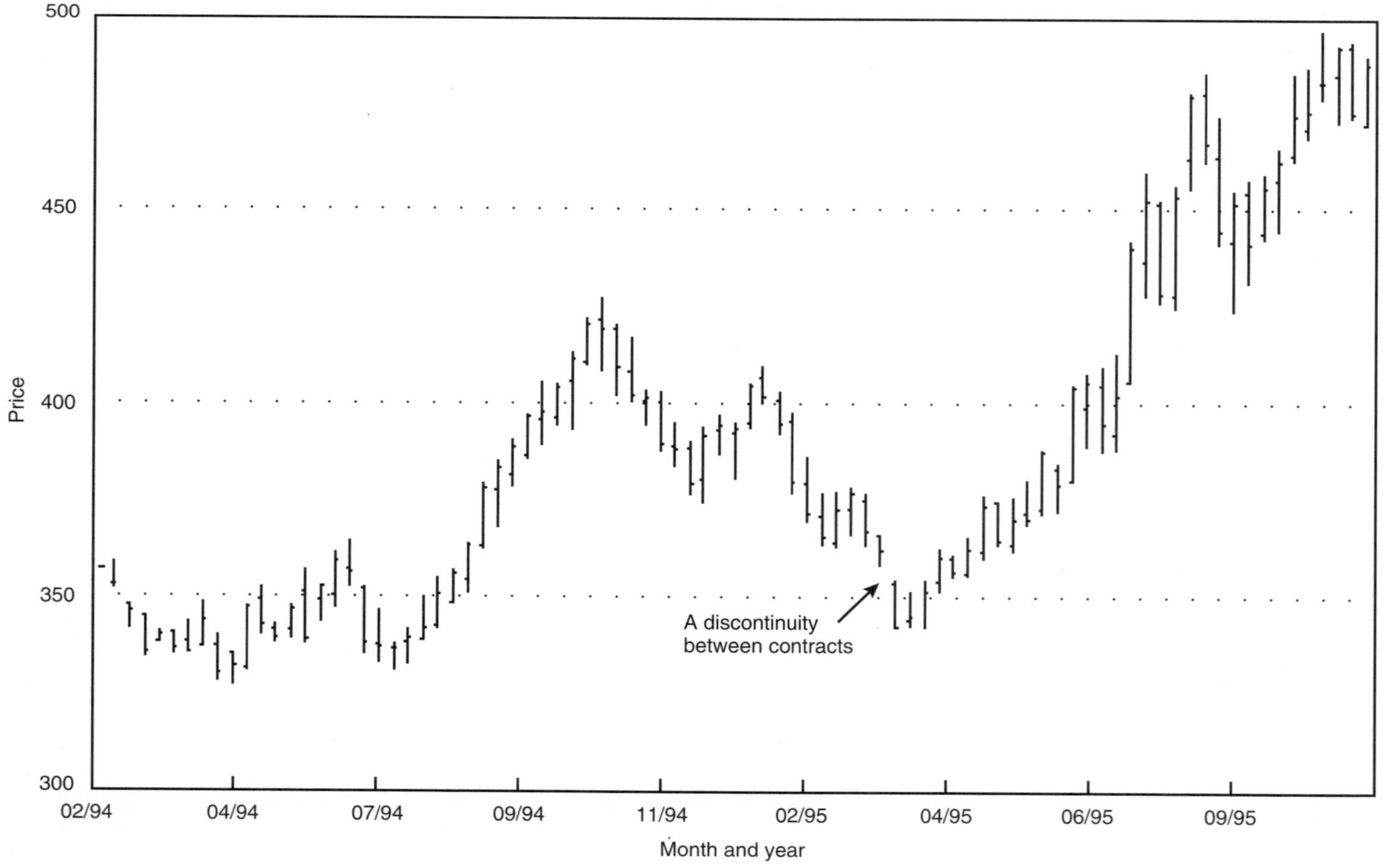

FIGURE 2-14

Monthly Chart of CBOT Wheat, 1986 to October, 1995

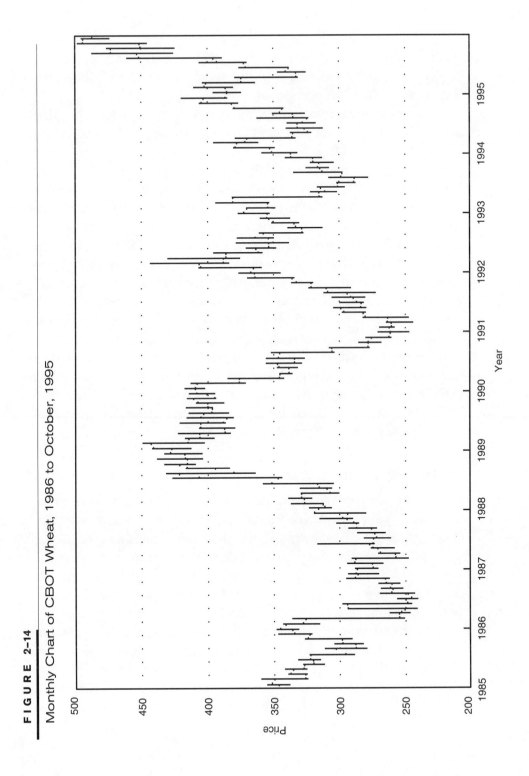

the year. Wheat, for example, often has less value at harvest time because so much is coming into the marketplace than it does after the harvest has been completed.

Price discontinuity within the same contract month is called a gap. Gaps arise from a sudden change in perceived supply or demand for a commodity.

Traders use charts to analyze the technical side of the market. They use the patterns that prices make on a chart, called formations, to predict the future course of the market. Technical analysis of prices, or chart reading, is an art. When viewing a chart containing historical prices, the price formations and what they mean are obvious. However, when you watch the daily development of a formation, it is generally unclear what the final formation will be. Individuals vary dramatically in their ability to read charts. It is common for skilled chart readers to draw different conclusions as the formations develop day by day.

There are numerous newsletters to help traders analyze the technical and fundamental aspects of commodity markets. Two excellent newsletters are *Trends in Futures,* edited by Glen Ring and *Chart Insight,* edited by Ken Seehusen. Both are published by Oster Communications, P.O. Box 6, Cedar Falls, IA 50613.

G. NATURAL MOVEMENT OF COMMODITY PRICES

Commodity prices, however, do move in patterns that occur time and time again. What are these patterns? Let's look at a typical chart, Figure 2–15, showing daily price movement of a portion of the 1995 December live cattle market. Three things stand out in this chart: (1) prices move from one general price level to another, (2) prices move in an oscillatory or wave-like pattern, and (3) day-to-day price movement is quite erratic.

To make money in commodity speculation using classical technical techniques, such as chart reading, you need to know two things: the direction of price movement and the price of either a top or a bottom. To a limited extent, the direction of price movement can be predicted. Unfortunately, the prices of tops and bottoms defy accurate prediction.

FIGURE 2-15

1995 December Live Cattle from 3/1/95 to 10/17/95

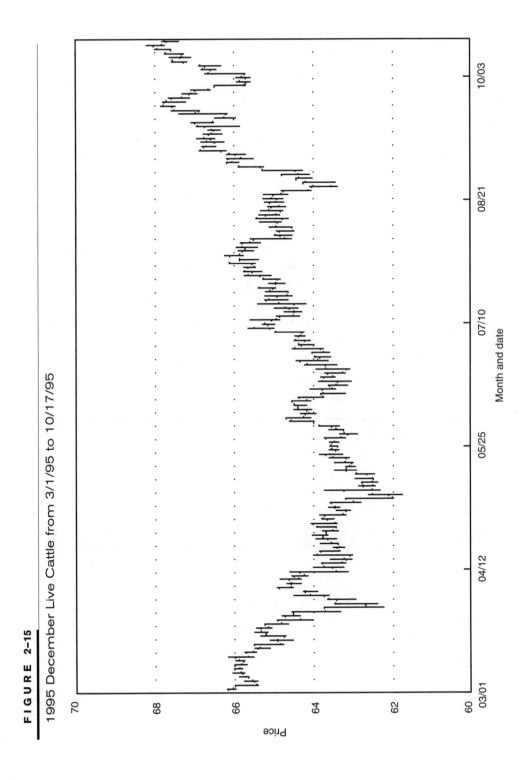

What can we predict about future market action? For any
commodity, there are only two things we can predict with any de-
gree of accuracy:

1. The price will move in trends.

2. The price will move in a wave-like cycle.

The Price Moves in Trends

Although the day-to-day price change is extremely erratic, when
the price pattern is taken as a whole, trends usually become apparent. A trend is an erratic but general movement of prices from
one level to another. The major trends of a market are related to
supply and demand. Inspection of any commodity chart will show
price trends. A fairly lengthy uptrend can be seen in the chart of
1995 December live cattle (Figure 2–15). The trend started in
April 1995 with a low of about 62 and moved to a high of about 68
during October 1995.

The duration of trends forms a continuum from extremely
short (minutes) to extremely long (decades). Trends can be seen in
the intraday market charts, in daily charts, and in yearly charts.
For our purposes, we will define three types of trends based upon
their duration: (1) short-term, lasting one day to several weeks;
(2) intermediate, lasting several weeks to several months; and
(3) long-term, lasting from several months to several years. These
are not precise definitions but will be adequate for our purposes.

The duration of a trend is not related to the price movement
within the trend. The price movement within a trend can vary
from drastic to flat (sideways or no change in price). Short-term,
intermediate, and long-term trends can all have drastic to flat
price movements.

We can state, without qualification, that future commodity
prices will move in trends. We can also state, without qualification, that we will not be able to accurately predict the duration of
these trends nor the extent of the price movement within the
trend. Fortunately, we do not need to know either of these for successful Interval Trading. However, the types of trends a market is
experiencing do affect the profitability of Interval Trading.

FIGURE 2–16

Price Oscillations in a Market

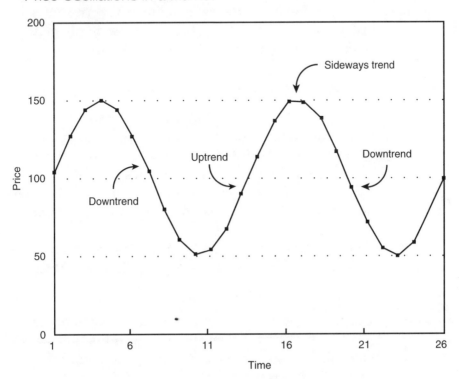

The Market Moves in Wave-Like Cycles

Regardless of the type of trend, the market moves in a wave-like pattern (see Figure 2–16). In fact, trends can be construed to be a part of the wave-like pattern, or cycle, found in the market. When evaluating a commodity chart, you will find waves within waves within waves. (For those of you who are mathematicians, the mathematical concept of chaos will leap to mind.)

We will call these wave-like patterns "oscillations." Some oscillations can be correlated with reports on fundamental factors, such as supply and demand. Other oscillations can be correlated with technical factors, such as an oversold or overbought condition of the market. The small, day-to-day oscillations result from all of these factors being felt in the marketplace, but in such small amounts that the pattern appears to be random.

While all markets have oscillations, the time period between lows (troughs) and highs (crests) is extremely erratic. While commodity oscillations have a sine-wave shape, they are not sine waves, and they do not lend themselves to precise mathematical analysis as do electrical, light, or radio waves.

H. PREDICTING COMMODITY PRICE MOVEMENTS

Techniques (also called *systems, methods,* or *trading strategies*) to predict price movement abound. As you might imagine, there are literally hundreds of different techniques, many of which are for sale. Some have very impressive track records. Almost all of these trading techniques work—at least part of the time. To the authors' knowledge, there is no system that works all of the time.

The different trading techniques can be classified into two major groups: trend-following methods, and oscillation methods.

Trend-Following Methods

Trading methods based upon direction of price movement are called *trend-following methods*. The operative word is "following." These methods all follow a trend and attempt to determine, by using price alone, if the trend is continuing in the same direction or has changed direction. A moving average is the classical trend-following method. With a moving average system, you buy contracts when the price closes above the moving average and sell them when the close is below it. Since Interval Trading does not use a moving average, we will refer you to John J. Murphy, *Technical Analysis of the Futures Markets* (New York Institute of Finance), for a description of a moving average, how it is calculated, and how it is used in trading commodity markets.

One major disadvantage of trend-following methods is that they cannot predict a top or a bottom. Consequently, you must wait for prices to move in the reverse direction for a certain amount of time (or price) before the system signals that the trend changed direction.

Another major disadvantage of trend-following methods is that they require a reasonably large advance or decline in prices to be profitable. If the prices move sideways, which they do a considerable portion of the time, a trend-following method will cause you to lose money by having you repeatedly reverse your position with small- to medium-sized losses (an activity called *whipsaw*).

Oscillation Methods

The wave-like pattern of commodity price movement provides the basis of Cyclic Analysis of Commodities and the Elliott Wave Theory. The underlying concept of these approaches is that there is sufficient periodicity within the wave pattern that the waves can be used for trading. Oscillators, such as price momentum, stochastics, and RSI (relative strength indicator), are based upon the fact that commodities move in wave-like patterns. The terms *overbought* and *oversold* are used to describe the extremes in oscillations.

Cyclic Analysis has been described in detail in the book *The Handbook of Commodity Cycles* by Jake Bernstein (New York: Ronald Press, John Wiley and Sons, 1982). Cyclic analysis is also the basis of Walter Bressert's excellent 1991 book *The Power of Oscillator/Cycle Combinations* and his computer programs *CycleFinder* and *CycleTrader* (P.O. Box 8068, Vero Beach, Florida 32963). For anyone who is seriously interested in commodity trading, these books and programs are a must.

The Elliott Wave Theory is based upon the observation that the major trend in a commodity market often consists of five major waves: three in the direction of the trend and two counter to it.

I. THE BASIC TRADING STRATEGIES—GOING LONG AND GOING SHORT

There must be a change in price for the commodity trader to make money. It is possible to make money if prices go up or if prices go down, but not if prices remain the same and move in a sideways fashion.

Long

The trading strategy for a price increase is called a *long*. Going long is a bullish strategy. When you have gone long or have a long position, you have bought the contract and are holding it in anticipation of a price increase. Going long is the trading strategy used in Interval Trading.

> Long: buy then sell; anticipate a price increase

When people think about buying stocks, bonds, etc. they naturally consider a long strategy. When you buy 100 shares of XYZ Corporation and hold those shares for several years expecting the stock to increase in value, you are using a long strategy. Collecting anything—stamps, art, wine, etc.—is a long strategy. You expect to hold the article until the price has increased and then sell it for a profit. The same strategy is used in commodities. You buy a contract, say of wheat (5,000 bushels), hold it for a period of time, then sell (offset) it. If the price has gone up, you will make a profit.

There are some differences between taking a long position in stocks and a long position in commodities. Most significant are the following:

1. *Time You Can Hold the Investment*   You can hold a stock certificate practically forever. Not so with a commodity futures contract. You will have to sell your commodity futures contract before its expiration date, whether you make or lose money.

2. *Margin*   You can buy stocks on margin, but the margin is relatively high (50 percent or greater). When you buy stocks on margin, you are really borrowing the difference between the amount you pay as a down payment and the full purchase price. The money for the margin is borrowed from the brokerage firm and you will have to pay interest on this borrowed money.

This is not the case with commodity futures contracts. Commodity margins are around 5 percent and you pay no interest. Commodity margin is not a down payment; it is earnest money for a purchase to be made in the future. As a speculator, you do not plan to accept delivery nor does anyone expect you to do so. There is no need to borrow money for the difference between the margin amount and the full value of the futures contract because you will never own the physical item.

Let's illustrate the margin differences with specific examples. Suppose you buy 1,000 shares of a $15 stock on 50 percent margin (total purchase $15,000). You will pay the brokerage firm $7,500 at the time of the purchase and borrow $7,500 from the brokerage firm at the current rate of interest.

When you buy a contract of wheat (5,000 bushels) for $3.00 a bushel, the total value of the contract is also $15,000. The margin you will deposit with the brokerage firm is about $675 and you pay no interest on the $15,000. The difference is that you have not bought the wheat. You would do so only at time of delivery. What you have bought is the contractual obligation to accept and pay for the wheat at the time of delivery. The $675 is only earnest money for this obligation, not a down payment on a purchase.

3. *Certificates* When you purchase a stock, you can request and receive stock certificates. There is no comparable certificate in commodity trading. Your only paper trail will be the accounting reports you receive from your brokerage firm.

4. *Money Needed* The amount of money needed to purchase a stock depends upon its price. You will need $2,000 to purchase 100 shares of a $20 stock and $5,000 for 100 shares of a $50 stock. This is not the case with commodities. The amount of money you will need to deposit for the purchase of a commodity contract is independent of the price of the commodity itself. If wheat is selling for $3.00 a bushel or if wheat is selling for $4.00 a bushel, you will need the same amount of money for the margin deposit—about $675. The difference, again, is that margin is earnest money, not a down payment. You buy stocks in the stock market. You buy an obligation in the commodity market.

5. *Commissions* To purchase a stock or a commodity, you must work through a broker who will charge you a commission for his or her services (see Chapter 9). The commission you will pay a stockbroker is based upon the price of the stock. The higher the price of the stock, the greater the commission. This is not true for commodities. A commodity broker charges a fixed commission that is independent of the price of the commodity. The actual dollar value of the commission will vary from commodity to com-

modity and from broker to broker. In general, you can expect to
pay anywhere from $25 to $50 per transaction (a buy or a sell)
per contract.

Since going long will be our principal strategy in Interval
Trading, let's go through a specific example of a long transaction
to ensure that the mechanics are clear.

Example:

You tell your broker to buy one contract (reported to you as 5,000
bushels) of December wheat at the market. (You are going to go
long December wheat and buy it at the price for which it is being
traded when your order reaches the floor broker.) Your broker en-
ters the order with his or her commission house. Once the order is
filled, he or she reports back to you. For example, "You purchased
December wheat at 301 1/2." All of these transactions are carried
out by phone.

Let's assume that, several weeks after your purchase, the price
of wheat has gone up and you have decided to take profit. To do
this you sell (offset) a contract of December wheat. (It has to be a
sale of December wheat to offset your long December wheat contract. Selling a September or a May wheat will not offset your long
December position.) Let's assume your offsetting sale was made at
330 1/2 and that your broker's commission was $50 for the round-
turn (the purchase and sale).

Calculations:

Offset (sold) at:	330 1/2
Long (purchase) at:	301 1/2
Difference:	29 cents
At $50 per cent:	× $50
Gross:	$1450
Less commissions:	<$50>
Net profit:	$1400

Short

The trading strategy for a price decline is called a *short*. Going
short is a bearish strategy. When you have gone short or have a
short position, you have sold the contract and are waiting for a

price decline. When the price is low enough, you will buy a contract to offset your sale. Going short is *not* used in Interval Trading; therefore, it will be discussed only briefly.

Short: sell then buy; anticipate a price decline

Going short is equivalent to a retail merchant selling an article to a customer for a fixed price, anticipating that he or she can purchase the article in the future for much less. The article is sold to the customer before it is purchased. Similarly, in commodity trading a contract can be sold before it is purchased. The trader will profit if the price of the commodity declines.

Example:

While holding no long contracts, you sell December wheat at 301 1/2. Therefore, you have gone short at 301 1/2. Assume that, after several weeks, the price has declined to 290 1/4. You offset your short position by buying a December wheat contract. Commissions for short positions are the same as for long positions; assume it to be $50.

Calculations:

Sold short at:	301 1/2
Offset purchase at:	290 1/4
Difference:	11 1/4
At $50 per cent:	× $50
Gross:	$562.50
Less commissions:	<$50>
Net:	$512.50

Interval Trading:
An Introduction

We can accurately predict only three things about the future price action of an agricultural commodity:

1. Prices will not go to zero.
2. Prices will move in trends.
3. Prices will oscillate.

These market characteristics form the basis of Interval Trading. Unlike other trading methods, to successfully Interval Trade you need not know the price of a future top or bottom nor when either will occur.

A. THE PRICE OF A MAJOR COMMODITY WILL NOT GO TO ZERO

We have discussed trends and oscillations in Chapter 2. Now we will discuss the basic tenet of Interval Trading: the price of a basic agricultural commodity will not go to zero.

A corporation can go bankrupt; a commodity, such as wheat, will not. The price of a stock or a bond can drop to zero if the underlying business fails, but a commodity is not a business like a corporation. Rather they are raw materials produced by businesses and sold in a free and open marketplace. If the price of a basic commodity drops low enough, the producers of that commodity may go bankrupt, but the commodity itself won't become worthless.

FIGURE 3–1

The Lower Level of a Commodity Price

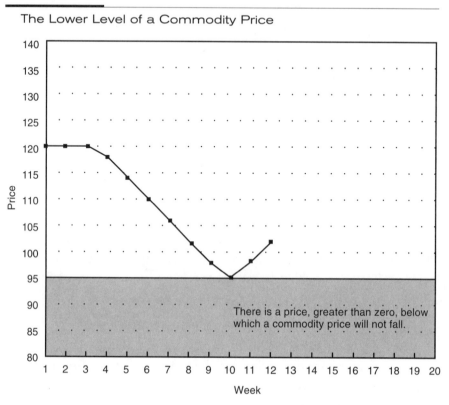

The value of an agricultural commodity is determined by supply and demand. If the supply is large, prices will drop; if demand exceeds supply, prices rise. However, the price of a commodity never goes to zero. Consequently, we can predict that the lower prices go, the greater the chances that a price rally will follow. This is a fundamental tenet of Interval Trading. As the price of the commodity drops lower and lower, the probability of a price rally increases (see Figure 3–1). A rough analogy is a compression spring. As the spring is compressed, the forces pushing against the compression increase. As the price of a commodity decreases, supplies will decrease, and the demand will increase. The two forces of supply and demand, working in conjunction, will eventually drive the price upward.

While it is possible to predict the absolute lower limit of a price decline (zero), it is impossible to predict the absolute upper limit of prices during a time of great shortage. How high is up? In times of true shortage, the price of a commodity can increase without bound and without any relationship to its historical upper price levels. There is no natural limit on rising prices. Therefore, we don't use short sales in Interval Trading. We trade only from the long side of the market. We buy long positions when prices are relatively low and sell them in the ensuing rally.

Index futures, interest rate futures, and the currencies are not as free to respond to the cycle of supply and demand as are the agricultural or industrial (energies and metals) commodities. In some respects, the financial futures are controlled by governments for political purposes. Consequently, we do not Interval Trade the financial futures.

B. INTERVAL TRADING—THE BASIC IDEA

Trading methods can be classified into two major groups:

1. Those that take advantage of trends.

2. Those that take advantage of oscillations.

Both groups of trading methods attempt to predict a bottom (or top) and trade accordingly. Interval Trading belongs to both groups of techniques. However, Interval Trading differs from all other methods in that there is no attempt to accurately predict a bottom or top.

> Interval Trading is the purchase of long positions at fixed, predetermined levels (the interval) in a declining or bottoming market. Profit is taken in a subsequent rising market.

To explain the basic concept of Interval Trading, let's use a line drawing of a commodity making a bottom with a V pattern (Figure 3–2). (A V-bottom is only one of the many types of bottom

FIGURE 3–2

Hypothetical V-Bottom Market

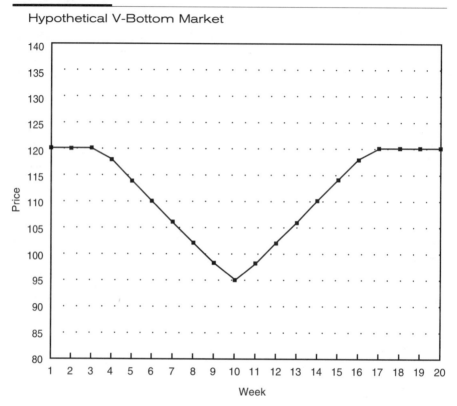

formations observed in commodity charts.) Assume that the commodity has been trading in the 120-point range and then declines
over a period of 10 weeks to the 95-point range, at which point it
reverses its trend and returns to the 120-point range. For simplicity, we will concentrate on the up and down trends and ignore oscillations that would also occur during these trends. This, of
course, is not a real example, but allows us to explain how Interval Trading works.

For our example, we will set the upper level for trading at
120 and our trading interval at 10 points. These two values determine our purchase prices. Before the first long contract is purchased, we also calculate our offset prices. These are the prices at
which we will offset our long positions for a profit. In this example, we use a 10-point profit target. Therefore, each offset price or

TABLE 3-1

An Interval-Trading Table
(Upper Trading Level, 120; Interval, 10 Points)

Purchase Long at	Sell Offset at	Profit Target
110	120	10
100	110	10
90	100	10
80	90	10
		Potential profit = 40

target price is 10 points higher than its purchase price. These three parameters are the basic variables in Interval Trading:

1. The top price for trading (upper trading level).
2. The interval between purchases (the interval).
3. The profit target.

Once we have selected values for our three variables, we can assemble our Interval-Trading table (see Table 3–1).

Figure 3–3 shows the application of the Interval table to the V-bottom market. The first contract was purchased at 110 during week 6 and then sold 11 weeks later (during week 17) at 120. The second contract was purchased during week 8 at 100 and sold 6 weeks later (during week 14) at 110. Both contracts showed a profit of 10 points for a total profit of 20 points.

In this hypothetical Interval Trade, we were prepared to buy additional contracts at 90 and at 80 but the market never dropped to those levels.

This type of trading activity will be successful only if you are assured of a price rally after a decline. *In order to buy and hold long positions in a declining market, you will have to firmly believe a price rally is about to follow.*

Once trading has started, the extent of the price decline prior to the rally determines the drawdown and capital needed for successful Interval Trading. Obviously, the closer a market is to a major bottom when we start our Interval Trading, the lower will be our capital needs to cover drawdown. We will discuss these topics in greater detail in the chapters that follow.

FIGURE 3–3

Two Interval Trades in a V-Bottom Market

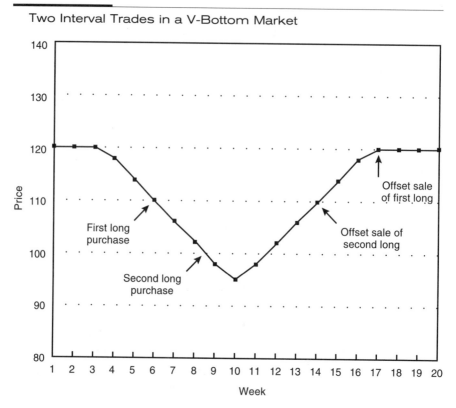

C. APPLICATION OF AN INTERVAL TABLE TO A REAL MARKET

Before continuing, let's apply an Interval table to a real market (July 1993 frozen orange juice). We will use the period from 12/7/92 to 6/23/93 (see Figure 3–4). The trades in this hypothetical example could have been made, but like all real-market examples in this book, they were not taken by these authors. All real-market examples have been chosen with hindsight in order to illustrate and explain Interval Trading.

In viewing the daily chart in Figure 3–4 as a whole, we can see orange juice made a V-bottom in early February 1993. On the chart, prices started their downtrend around 105 ($1.05 per lb). The decline terminated near 75. On the way down, there were two minor oscillations. Numerous other oscillations can be observed in the chart.

FIGURE 3-4

Two Hypothetical Interval Trades in July 1993 Frozen Orange Juice (12/7/92 to 6/23/93)

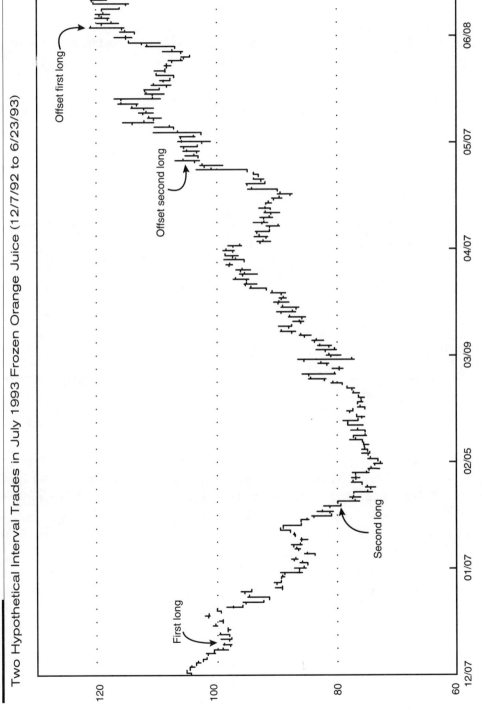

TABLE 3-2

Hypothetical Scale Trading of July 1993 Frozen Orange Juice*

Purchase of Long		Offset Sale		
Price	Date	Price	Date	Profit/<loss>
100.00	12/11/92	120.00	6/22/93	20.00
80.00	1/27/93	100.00	5/10/93	20.00
				Total:40.00
			Dollar value $6000.00	

*The calculation of the dollar value from points can be confusing. In the case of frozen orange juice, the minimum fluctuation is 0.05 cents/pound ($0.0005/pound), which is 5 points/pound. A contract of frozen orange juice contains 15,000 lbs. Therefore, the minimum fluctuation is equal to 15,000 pounds × $0.0005/pound or $7.50. One point is consequently worth ($7.50/5) or $1.50. A price change of $0.40 is thus equal to $6000: ($0.40/$0.00050) × $7.50. A second way to make the calculation is that $0.40 cents is 4000 points; 4000 points × $1.50 per point = $6000. A third way to make the calculation is that each 1-cent price change ($0.01 or 100 points) is equal to $150. Therefore, a 40-cent price change is equal to 40 × $150 or $6000.

Applying the interval we used with our hypothetical V-bottom market (Table 3–1), we would have made the trades listed in Table 3–2.

D. DRAWDOWN

A contract of frozen orange juice contains 15,000 lbs. Therefore, a profit of 4,000 points ($0.4000 per pound) is $6,000 (1 point = $1.50; see the footnote in Table 3–2 for an explanation). What is the percent return on your margin? The initial margin for orange juice is about $1,000. Since two contracts were held during the same interval period, the total initial margin requirements would have been $2,000. Consequently, the percent return is 300 percent [($6,000/$2,000) × 100].

However, you would need considerably more money to carry out this interval trade. In the real world, the capital requirements for Interval Trading are more complex than this simple calculation would lead you to believe. The problem is *drawdown*, the amount of money needed to cover the price decline as the market proceeds towards its bottom (see Figure 3–5). We will consider this topic very briefly here and then revisit it in detail in the next chapter, Chapter 4.

FIGURE 3-5

Drawdown and Profit in Interval Trading

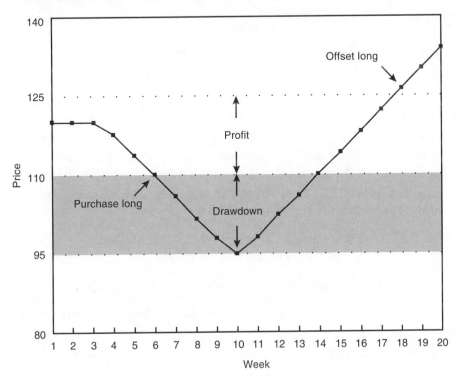

You must have sufficient funds in your account to cover the price decline of all commodity futures contracts you own. If you have not deposited sufficient funds to cover the price declines, you will be asked to deposit more funds (a margin call). Since, in a real-world market, we have no idea where the bottom will be, we must have sufficient funds to cover all contingencies.

Let us make the calculation of the amount of drawdown for this orange juice market using after-the-fact information. To carry the contracts to the market low of 72.60 on 2/9/93, you would have needed $5,200.

Drawdown for the First Long Purchase:
        100.00 (purchase price) − 72.60 (market low)
        = 27.40 (difference)
        = $0.2740 per lb or 2,740 points

Drawdown for the Second Long Purchase:

$$80.00 \text{ (purchase price)} - 72.60 \text{ (market low)}$$
$$= 7.40 \text{ (difference)}$$
$$= \$0.0740 \text{ or } 740 \text{ points}$$

Total Drawdown for both Contracts:

$$2,740 \text{ points} + 740 \text{ points} = 3,480 \text{ points}$$

A price fluctuation of 1,000 points ($0.10 per lb) in the price of an orange juice contract (15,000 lbs) equals $1,500. Therefore, 3,480 points equals $5,220. This is the amount of money needed to cover the drawdown of the two orange juice contracts. In addition, you would need the margin for the two contracts, which would total $2,000. Therefore, the total amount of money or the capital needed is:

$$\text{Margin} + \text{Drawdown} = \text{Capital needed}$$
$$\$2,000 + \$5,220 = \$7,220$$

A closer estimate of our real percent return is:

$$[(\$6,000/\$7,220) \times 100] = 83\%$$

This value is considerably less than 300 percent, but still nothing to complain about.

It is important to note that the money you need on deposit is not being spent, but it must be in the hands of the broker's commission house. You will not be paid interest on the amount of the funds needed for drawdown. While the money has not actually been spent, it still is at risk. Should you find it necessary to liquidate your positions, the money will be gone (not the money used for margin; just the money required to cover the drawdown).

In the real market, we don't know what the price of a bottom will be as the market drops toward it. We have to guess where it might be. It is one thing to trade historical data where you know what the result will be and a completely different thing to watch your account value plummet as the market drops toward a bottom you know is down there—somewhere! Interval Trading is not for the undercapitalized speculator nor for the faint of heart. If you don't have sufficient funds to ride out the price decline, you

TABLE 3-3

Interval-Trading Table for 1995 Live Cattle
(Upper Trading Level, 65.50; Interval, 100 Points)

Purchase at	Offset at	Profit Target
64.50	65.50	1.00
63.50	64.50	1.00
62.50	63.50	1.00
61.50	62.50	1.00
	Potential profit: 400 points	

will be forced to liquidate near the bottom of the market with devastating losses. It is best not to start unless you can see it through.

E. OSCILLATION PROFITS

In an up- or downtrend, prices will rally against the trend. These price movements against a primary trend have several names, such as rallies, sell-offs, reactions, bulges, and oscillations. We will call them oscillations. A price trend and its oscillations form a wave-like pattern that is characteristic of a free market.

To illustrate how oscillations can be used for profit in Interval Trading, let us pretend we are Interval Trading December 1995 live cattle (Figure 3–6) using the Interval Table given in Table 3–3.

The upper trading level will be 65.00 cents per lb and the interval, 100 points ($0.01 per lb; 40,000 lb contract). Our profit target will also be 100 points. With live cattle, 100 points equals $400. For simplicity, we will restrict the trading period from 3/21/95 to 7/11/95. (Inspection of the chart in Figure 3–6 shows that after 7/11/95 several additional interval trades would have been successful. These were excluded from our example to decrease the arithmetic.)

With these parameters, we would have made the purchases and offsetting sales listed in Table 3–4.

FIGURE 3-6

1995 December Live Cattle (3/1/95 to 10/17/95)

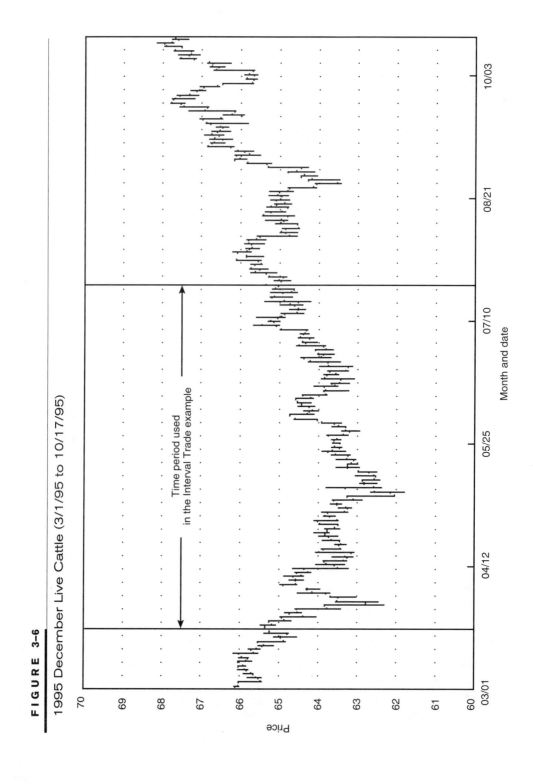

TABLE 3–4

Hypothetical Interval Trading of December 1995 Live Cattle
(3/21/95 to 7/11/95)

Purchase of Long		Offset Sale		
Price	Date	Price	Date	Profit/<loss>
64.50	3/24/95	65.50	7/7/95	100
63.50	3/28/95	64.50	4/4/95	100
62.50	3/29/95	63.50	3/30/95	100
63.50	4/11/95	64.50	6/5/95	100
62.50	5/8/95	63.50	5/10/95	100
62.50	5/11/95	63.50	5/17/95	100
63.50	6/14/95	64.50	6/29/95	100

Total: 700 points

Gross profit: $2800

A table of trades, such as that given in Table 3–4, is fine for accounting purposes but very unsatisfactory for illustrating the time sequence of trades. Therefore, consider the graph given in Figure 3–7, which should help clarify the trading sequence.

As you can see, prices did not go straight down then up, but oscillated as they approached and came off the bottom. When we use a properly sized interval, we can profit by buying and selling as these oscillations occur. In our example, 400 points ($1600) of the total 700 points ($2800) were oscillation profits. Oscillation profits provide a significant income for the Interval Trader.

Again, we wish to emphasize that while the trades illustrated in these examples were possible, the examples were chosen with hindsight to illustrate the concepts in Interval Trading.

F. IS INTERVAL TRADING THE SAME AS AVERAGING DOWN?

Averaging down and Interval Trading are similar but different market strategies. In both techniques, long contracts are purchased as prices drop. We will employ a modified form of averaging down in our rollover strategy (see Chapter 6), the strategy that we will use when the contract approaches its delivery date.

FIGURE 3-7

Sequence of Hypothetical Long Purchases and Offsetting Sales
Taken from Table 3-4

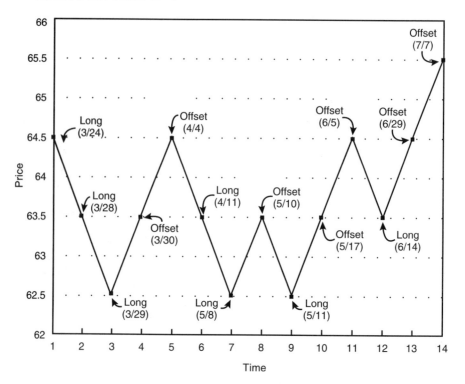

Averaging down and Interval Trading differ by how profits
are taken. In averaging down, the purchase prices of the contracts
are averaged. The desired profit is added to that average price to
obtain the target price. Profit is taken by the simultaneous sale of
all contracts at the target price. For example, suppose you make
purchases at 90, 80, and 70 in a dropping market (see Figure
3–8). The average price for these three contracts is 80 regardless
of how far the market goes below 70. For example, if the price
drops to 60 or even 50, your average purchase price is still 80.

If your profit objective is 10 points, then your profit target is
90—the average purchase price plus your profit objective. You
must sell all three contracts at 90 in order to make 10 points
profit on each of the three contracts (a total of 30 points profit).

FIGURE 3-8

Average Down Trading

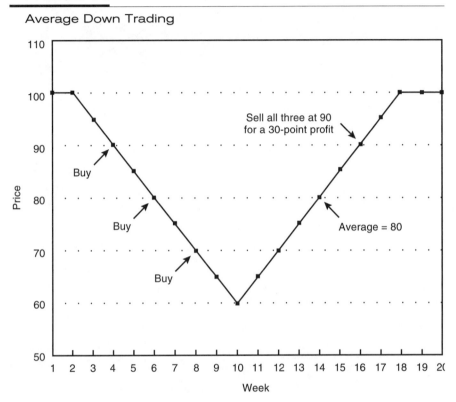

With Interval Trading, purchases would also be made at 90, 80, and 70. However, you would offset them in a different manner. Each contract is sold 10 points above its purchase price. There is no averaging. In Interval Trading, the contract purchased at 70 would be sold at 80, the contract purchased at 80 would be sold at 90, and so on.

The advantage of averaging down is that your target price is lower than it can be in Interval Trading. In the example given, the averaging-down positions were all offset at 90. In Interval Trading you would have to wait until the price was at 100 to offset your last contract.

The major advantage of Interval Trading is that oscillation profits can be taken, and these can be significant. In Interval Trading, one of the goals is to take as many oscillation profits as possible. Oscillation profits cannot be taken using an averaging-down strategy.

CHAPTER 4

Drawdown

Most retail stores carry an inventory of the articles they sell. These articles are purchased using capital or credit before they are sold. The inventory is an asset of the business, but it cannot be readily liquidated. Consequently, the owner of the business must balance the need for inventory against the other capital requirements, such as payroll. If the owner is careless, some inventory may have to be sold at a financial loss for liquidity.

Interval Trading, like a retail store, requires inventory. Contracts must be purchased before they can be sold. When purchasing contracts, the Interval Trader is, in effect, putting contracts into inventory. Like the retail store owner, the Interval Trader must use capital wisely. If the Interval Trader purchases too many contracts, or contracts at too high of a price, some of them may have to be sold at a financial loss to maintain liquidity.

When a retail merchant buys additional inventory, cash-on-hand decreases and the value of the inventory increases. When these two bookkeeping transactions are made, they offset one another and the net worth of the business remains the same. Assuming the inventory is neither sold nor depreciated, its book value will remain constant as long as the owner keeps it there. This is not true of an inventory consisting of commodity futures contracts. The value of a commodity futures contract fluctuates daily. Consequently, the value of the trader's account fluctuates daily.

The major differences between the inventory of a retail merchant and that of an Interval Trader arise from drawdown and rollovers. *Drawdown* is the decrease in value of a commodity futures contract due to price erosion. *Rollover* is the required sale of a contract at the end of its life and the subsequent purchase of another contract in a more distant month.

In Interval Trading, inadequate capital can arise from either drawdown itself or from drawdown followed by a rollover. Both drawdown and rollovers are normal in Interval Trading and must be planned for as part of the trading strategy. If the Interval Trader does not plan for both drawdown and rollovers, he or she could easily go broke.

We will discuss drawdown in this chapter and defer the discussion of rollovers until Chapter 5.

A. MARGIN

Let's identify the major components of the commodity account held by the broker's commission house. Purchase of a wheat contract, for example, requires an initial margin deposit. The amount of the initial margin varies depending upon the broker, the commission house, and the market conditions, but for our discussion, let's say it is $675.

The initial margin really represents earnest money for the obligations assumed in purchasing the contract. Initial margin is not a down payment on the contract.

If wheat is selling for $3.00 a bushel, then one contract of wheat (5,000 bushels) is worth $15,000. You will not be required to produce the full $15,000 unless you take delivery of the commodity, which speculators never do. Therefore, once the contract has been purchased, you are required to maintain an adequate balance in your account to cover your obligation against a price drop. This balance is called the maintenance margin, which is generally about 75 percent of the initial margin.

B. DRAWDOWN

The price of the commodity fluctuates every day. At the end of each day, the broker's commission house credits and debits each trader's account to reflect the change of all commodities prices held by the trader. If you hold a long position and the price of that commodity goes up, then the value of your account will be increased. However, if the price goes down, so does the value of your account. Again using wheat as an example, if the price per bushel goes up $0.10, then $500 is added to your account. If the price drops $0.10, then $500 is subtracted from your account.

If the price of the commodity goes up immediately after a long purchase, maintaining the account above the required maintenance margin is not a problem because more money is added to the account each day that the price goes up. However, if the price goes down immediately after purchase, then the dollar value of the account can easily slip under the maintenance margin level. If this occurs, your broker will issue a margin call—a polite request for more money. The amount of money requested will be sufficient to bring the account to its original margin level.

Let's work through an example so we can see the amount of money required for a margin call.

Example

Suppose we purchase a long position in wheat at 300 ($3.00 a bushel). Our initial margin was $675 and, after the purchase, our maintenance margin is $500. If the price of wheat decreases by 4 cents (to 296), we will get a margin call for $200 to bring the deposit up to its initial margin level. A price fluctuation of 4 cents is extremely common in wheat.

Calculations:

Initial purchase (long):	$3.00
Current price:	$2.96
Difference:	$0.04 or 4 points
At $50 per point:	×$50
Drawdown:	$200

In Interval Trading, our strategy is to buy long near a major bottom and sell those contracts as the market rises. Unfortunately, we can only estimate where the bottom might be. Therefore, we must have sufficient capital to cover all margin calls as the price decreases to its bottom. This amount of money is the drawdown.

Note that we are using the word "drawdown" to mean two things: (1) the amount of money by which our contract has actually decreased; and (2) the amount of money we will need in the future to cover the margin calls during the price drop to the market bottom. We can accurately calculate (1) but only estimate (2).

Though we do not know where or when the bottom will occur, we can make some rational guesses based upon historical data. Since a rational guess is still a guess, we must have sufficient capital as a buffer so we can sleep well at night.

In summary, the amount of money needed for each contract in an Interval Trade is:

Capital needed = Initial margin + Drawdown

The total amount of money needed for a successful Interval Trading account is the sum of the capital needs for all Interval-Traded commodities.

C. CALCULATION OF THE DRAWDOWN

Before we begin to Interval Trade a commodity, we must calculate what the drawdown might be. This is extremely difficult because we do not know where the bottom price will be. However, we can select a price and calculate how much money will be needed should the price drop to that level. The trick is to estimate the lowest price the commodity could sink to and make sure we have sufficient funds in the account to cover this amount of drawdown. It is prudent to have this amount plus an additional buffer in the account in case things go awry, which they often do.

We can make drawdown calculations by using a formula or by using a tabular (spreadsheet) method. Let's continue to use wheat for our example. Assume we are going to Interval Trade wheat using a 20-point interval along with an upper trading level of 300. The Interval Trading table is shown in Table 4–1.

Formula Calculation
The formula method is most useful when we want to calculate the drawdown for one contract. Select a price below the purchase price and calculate the drawdown to that level. For example, assume we purchased our first contract at 280. What will be the

TABLE 4-1

Interval Trading Table
(Upper Trading Level, 300; Interval, 20 Points)

Purchase at	Offset at
280	300
260	280
240	260
220	240
200	220

drawdown should the price erode to 260, the price of our second Interval purchase? The calculation is as follows:

Purchase price:	280
(less) Lower price:	<260>
Points decrease:	20
(multiplied by) Value per point:	× $50
Total drawdown for this contract:	$1000

We also can calculate the drawdown should the price erode to 240.

Purchase price:	280
(less) Lower price:	<240>
Points decrease:	40
(multiplied by) Value per point:	× $50
Total drawdown for this contract:	$2000

Similarly, we can calculate the drawdown to any price below the purchase price.

To get the total amount of money needed, we add the amount of margin to the drawdown. For example, if the initial margin is $675 and the prices erode to 260, prior to our purchase of the second contract we would need:

$$\text{Total amount of money needed} = \text{Margin} + \text{Drawdown}$$
$$= \$675 + \$1000$$
$$= \$1675$$

FIGURE 4-1

Layout for the Tabular Method of Calculating Drawdown

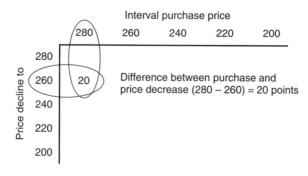

Tabular Calculations of Drawdown

A tabular method of calculating drawdown is more convenient when we must consider two or more contracts that have been purchased at different prices. To make a tabular calculation, lay out a box (matrix) that has a row of Interval purchase prices across the top and a column of declining prices down the side (see Figure 4–1).

Entries within the box are the difference between a row and a column value. For example, the box entry at 280 (Interval purchase price) and 260 (price-decline) is 20, the difference between 280 and 260. (If the difference is zero or a negative number, no entry is made in the box.)

Once all the box entries are filled, sum up the rows, then multiply each by the dollar value of one point. The resulting number is the total dollar amount of drawdown for all of the contracts purchased up to (but not including) that level.

Figure 4–2 contains a completed drawdown table for a 20-point Interval Trade for wheat from 300 (the upper trading level) to 200. (See Table 4–1 for the Interval Table.)

Inspection of Figure 4–2 shows that when prices have declined from 300 to 200, we have made purchases at 280, 260, 240, 220, but not yet at 200. Our total drawdown (in points) is the sum of the drawdown for each one of these positions. This value is obtained from the matrix by summing the numbers in the price decline row of 200. This total drawdown is 200 points or $10,000 for wheat, where one point is worth $50.

FIGURE 4–2

A 20-Point Drawdown Table for Wheat ($50 per Point)

Interval purchase price

	280	260	240	220	200	total	x $50
280	--	--	--	--	--	--	--
260	20	--	--	--	--	20	$1000
240	40	20	--	--	--	60	$3000
220	60	40	20	--	--	120	$6000
200	80	60	40	20	--	200	$10,000

Add these number to
get this sum

Multiply the sum by
the value of one point
of (wheat; $50) to get
the drawdown

Table 4–2, another drawdown table, shows the drawdown capital needed for Interval Trading when the upper trading level is 300 and the interval is 10 points. Inspection of this table shows that a price decline to 200 requires $22,500.

D. DRAWDOWN DEPENDS UPON THE INTERVAL

Inspection of Figure 4–2 and Table 4–2 raises an ugly fact: drawdown can be significant. Another fact, not quite so ugly, is:

The larger the interval between purchases, the smaller the drawdown.

By doubling the interval size from 10 to 20 points, the drawdown is reduced by about one-half at every level.

Interval Size	Drawdown from 300 to 200
10 points	$22,500
20 points	$10,000 (a 55% reduction)

TABLE 4-2

A 10-Point Drawdown Table for Wheat ($50 per point)

Price Decline to	290	280	270	260	250	240	230	220	210	200	Total	×$50
290	—	—	—	—	—	—	—	—	—	—	0	—
280	10	—	—	—	—	—	—	—	—	—	10	$500
270	20	10	—	—	—	—	—	—	—	—	30	$1,500
260	30	20	10	—	—	—	—	—	—	—	60	$3,000
250	40	30	20	10	—	—	—	—	—	—	100	$5,000
240	50	40	30	20	10	—	—	—	—	—	150	$7,500
230	60	50	40	30	20	10	—	—	—	—	210	$10,500
220	70	60	50	40	30	20	10	—	—	—	280	$14,000
210	80	70	60	50	40	30	20	10	—	—	360	$18,000
200	90	80	70	60	50	40	30	20	10	—	450	$22,500

Scale Purchase →

Potential drawdown is risk. The smaller the potential drawdown, the smaller the risk. Therefore, one significant technique
to reduce risk in Interval Trading is to use a reasonably large
interval.

Surprisingly, when we increase the interval size to reduce
risk, we do not significantly reduce our profit potential. Not surprisingly, we do reduce the number of trades. We will return to
this subject in Chapters 7 and 8.

CHAPTER 5

The Principal Variables in Interval Trading

In deciding to Interval Trade a commodity, you must make only three decisions:

1. Select the commodity.
2. Select the upper trading level.
3. Select the interval size.

The *selection of the commodity* is carried out using the principles of diversification. These principles are discussed in Chapter 11; therefore, we will defer a discussion of this subject until that chapter.

The *selection of the upper trading level* is the most important decision after the selection of the commodity. Unfortunately, there is no accurate method for choosing the upper trading level. If the selected level is too high, an excessive number of contracts could be purchased during a major decline. If the selected level is too low, you may never enter the market, or you may miss a significant number of oscillations. A compromise is needed.

The *selection of an interval size* can be quantified to an extent with historical data. In general, the interval size will be related to the commodity's price fluctuations (volatility). For example, soybeans are more volatile (make wider price fluctuations) than oats. A larger interval size must be used with soybeans than with oats. If the selected interval is too narrow, you may have numerous oscillation trades but accumulate an excessive number of

FIGURE 5-1

The Relationship Between Upper Trading Level, Interval, and the First Long Position

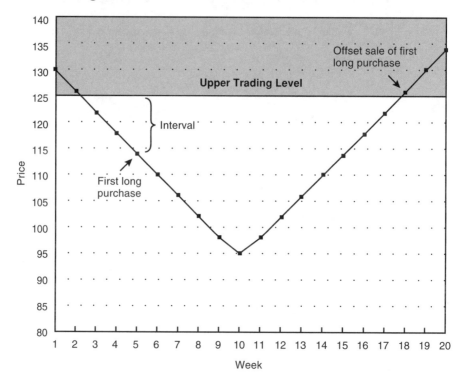

contracts during a market decline. If the interval is too large, you may not have any oscillation profits. As in the selection of the upper trading level, a compromise is required.

A. THE UPPER TRADING LEVEL DEFINED

Before discussing how to select the upper trading level, let's define the term. The upper trading level is the price at which we make our last offset sale. Therefore, the upper trading level is the price at which our inventory is cleared out at a profit and we cease to Interval Trade.

When we have selected the upper trading level and interval size, we then can identify the price of our first long purchase (see Figure 5–1).

Price of the first purchase = Upper trading level − Interval size

FIGURE 5-2

Interval Trading Versus Trend Following

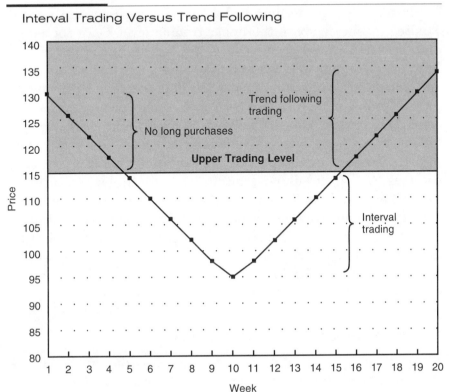

Note that we do not buy our first Interval Trade at the upper trading level. Rather, we will offset the last contract in our inventory at this level. If the price does not exceed the upper trading level by the end of the contract life, we will be forced to roll over a portion of our inventory.

In theory, we should take our first interval trade at one interval below the upper trading level. In practice, this can be too high of a price and expose us to a potentially large drawdown. From a purely pragmatic standpoint, we are better off to buy our first contract as close to a major bottom as possible. By doing so, our potential drawdown will be minimized. The sell-buy technique described in Chapter 7 will allow us to continue to Interval Trade and capture oscillation profits up to the upper trading level.

We do not Interval Trade above the upper trading level. Does this mean we never trade above the upper trading level? Of course we might, but it won't be Interval Trading. Consider the diagram in Figure 5-2.

The upper trading level defines the upper bounds for Interval Trading. During the decline, we take no long positions for Interval Trading inventory above the upper trading level. Once the prices drop below the upper trading level, we can begin our program of Interval Trading if we wish and take long purchases according to our plan. When prices move above the upper-trading level, our Interval-Trading inventory will be empty. At this point, a major uptrend may be underway. If we wish to continue to trade, we can take positions using a trend-following method or the sell-buy technique described in Chapter 7. However, our trading strategy changes. Above the upper trading level we no longer Interval Trade, but that doesn't mean we shouldn't trade. We just stop accumulating additional contracts when the market starts to drop.

In this book, we will restrict our discussion to Interval Trading. We will not discuss the tactics you could use for a transition from Interval Trading to a trend-following method, nor will we discuss which trend-following method you should use.

B. THE OPTIMUM UPPER TRADING LEVEL

An optimum upper trading level is defined as the price at which there is maximum profit and minimum drawdown. When viewing historical data, the selection of an optimum upper trading level tends to be a judgment call. The problem revolves around the relative importance of profit versus drawdown. As a result, two individuals may select two different optimum upper trading levels from the same historical data.

Each contract of each commodity for each year will have an optimum upper trading level. No two will be the same. Once this fact is accepted, the search for an all-inclusive upper trading level can be discarded. There will not be one upper trading level suitable for all contracts of a commodity, such as wheat, that can be used year in and year out.

To illustrate this point, consider the data contained in Table 5–1, the optimum upper trading levels for two contracts of wheat over a period of 10 years. As you can see, the values fluctuate considerably from one contract to the other in the same year, as well as from year to year.

TABLE 5-1

Optimum Upper Trading Levels for July and December Wheat*

Year	July Contract	December Contract
1983	365	375
1984	375	365
1985	340	360
1986	290	305
1987	285	295
1988	385	420
1989	410	420
1990	355	285
1991	320	360
1992	375	370
1993	310	—

*An interval of 25 points (see Table 5–4) and a sell-buy strategy (see Chapter 7) were used.

In order to Interval Trade, we must select a suitable upper trading level for the contract we wish to trade. Before becoming enmeshed in the mechanics of estimating an upper trading level, let's make sure we know where we are going and why it will only be a guess, no matter what we do. In selecting an upper trading level, we are trying to predict the future price of a commodity six months to a year in advance, an impossible task at best. What we need to determine is a price above which the market will rise by at least one "tick," the minimum price fluctuation for that commodity. We do not need to pick a top but we do need to pick a level (see Figure 5–3).

To select the upper trading level, we will use a two-step approach:

1. We will determine a benchmark value using historical data.
2. We then will adjust the benchmark value for the current market conditions (fundamentals, direction of market trend, etc.).

Since we are dealing with historical data in step 1, we can be reasonably sure of our value. With step 2, however, we are pre-

F I G U R E   5-3

Selecting an Upper Trading Level

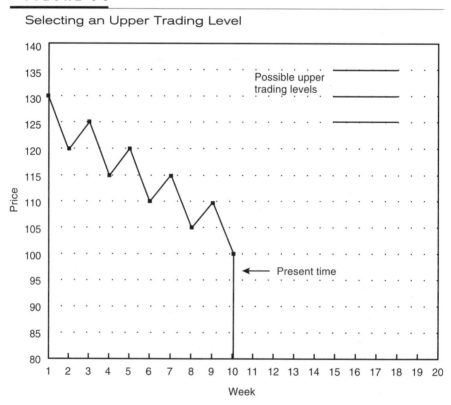

dicting the future. Consequently, we can never be assured that our value is correct until after the fact.

C. THE UPPER TRADING LEVEL: HISTORICAL ANALYSIS

A benchmark value for an upper trading level can be determined from historical analysis by using a monthly chart or simply by using a list of the highs and lows for the last 10 years. (See Chapter 10 for examples using just the highs and lows.)

Construct or obtain a monthly chart of a commodity with at least 10 years of data. By visual inspection of the chart, you will, in general, be able to categorize the chart as having (a) a sideways trend, (b) an uptrend, or (c) a downtrend over a 10-year period. If not over a complete 10-year period, then at least several years preceding the current month. Your categorization is subjective, but will be sufficient for our needs.

Charts with a 10-Year Sideways Trend

Consider the monthly chart for live hogs, Figure 5–4.

In looking at the chart, we can see that hogs have traded during the last 10 years from a high of about 67 in 1990 to a low of about 32 in 1994. Within this 10-year period, hog prices have remained rather flat, with oscillations from about 40 to 60.

For a flat market, we want to make our first Interval-Trade purchase at approximately the start of the lower one-third of the 10-year range. A very simple way to calculate this value is to take a third of the difference between the 10-year high and low and add it to the 10-year low value. Assuming the trading interval for hogs to be 4.00 points (see Section E of this chapter and Table 5–4 for an explanation of why this value was selected), the calculation of the benchmark value upper trading level follows:

Highest value:	66.975 (May 1990)
Lowest value:	31.600 (November 1994)
Difference:	35.375
1/3 of the difference:	11.79
Add to the low:	31.600 + 11.79 = 43.390
First purchase at:	43.00 (rounded down)
Upper trading level:	43.00 + 4.00 (assumed interval) = 47.00

Another way to calculate the one-third value is to use the last major top and bottom for the two extreme values rather than the 10-year high and low.

Last major top:	57.000 (March 1993)
Last major bottom:	31.600 (November 1994)
Difference:	25.400
1/3 of the difference:	8.466
Add to the low:	31.600 + 8.466 = 40.06
First purchase:	40.00 (rounded down)
Upper trading level:	40.00 + 4.00 (assumed interval) = 44.00

FIGURE 5-4

Monthly Live Hogs

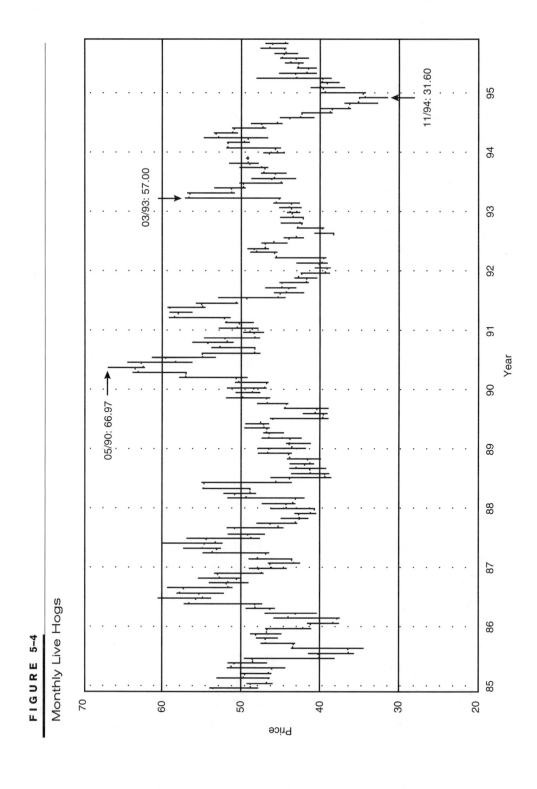

As you can see, both methods of calculation give about the same value, somewhere between 47 (aggressive) and 44 (conservative).

Charts with a 10-Year Downtrend

The straightforward method just works only if the long-term trend is relatively flat. If it is not flat, then the one-third procedure won't work.

As of this writing, none of the commodity markets recommended for trading (Table 1–1) has a price pattern showing a downward point market over a complete 10-year period. Therefore, to illustrate the point discussed here, let's use the 10-year cocoa chart covering the period from 1983 to 1993. Inspection of this chart (Figure 5–5) shows us the price was in a major downtrend for an extended period of time. In this type of market, the selection of an upper trading level using the lower one-third method will simply not work. Until the market has flattened, or at least until the downward trend is broken, you probably should not Interval-Trade this type of market. (During 1993, cocoa broke the long-term down trendline and afterward turned into a flat market, thus making it a candidate for Interval Trading.)

Charts with a 10-Year Uptrend

At the time of this writing, none of the commodities recommended for Interval Trading show a 10-year uptrend. (Although not recommended for Interval Trading, the S&P 500 does show such a trend.) To illustrate the method of calculation, the 10-year monthly chart for live cattle is given in Figure 5–6. Using the interval of 4.00 taken from Table 5–4, the calculation of the upper trading level follows:

Highest value:	84.30 (3/93)
Lowest value:	49.86 (6/86)
Difference:	34.44
1/3 of the difference:	11.48
Add to the low:	49.86 + 11.48 = 61.34
First purchase at:	61.00 (rounded down)
Upper trading level:	61.00 + 4.00 (assumed interval) = 65.00

FIGURE 5-5

10-Year Monthly Cocoa Chart

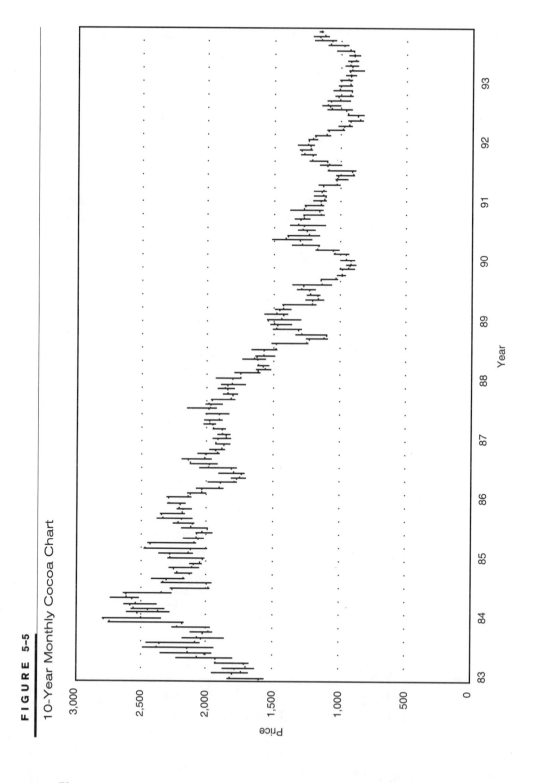

10-Year Monthly Live Cattle

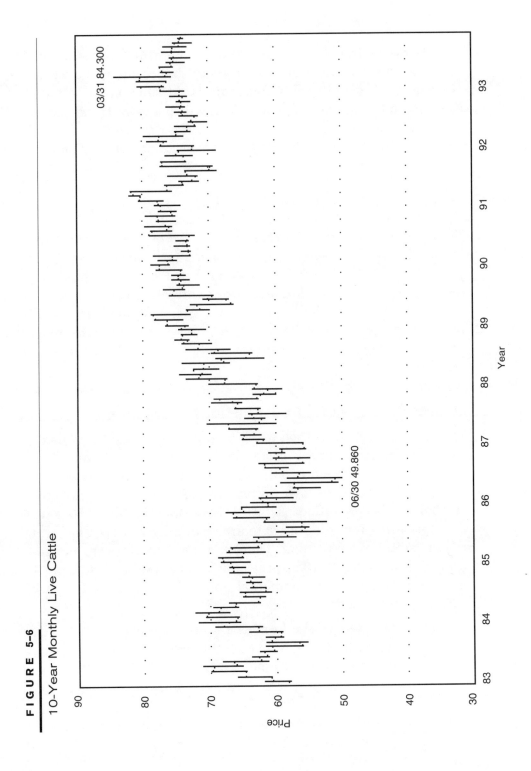

Be aware that Interval Trading a commodity in a 5 to 10-year uptrend is considerably more risky than trading one whose 10-year chart is reasonably flat market. At some point in time, the uptrend will end and the prices will begin to trend down. There is considerably more price difference between the most recent lows and the market's 10-year low in an uptrending market than is found in a flat market.

An Exponential Uptrend Market

There is one type of uptrending market you should never Interval Trade—the exponential uptrend market. An exponential uptrend market is moving upward at an increasing rate. The 1994 coffee is a classic example of an exponential market. Figure 5–7 shows the daily pattern of this market just prior to its collapse.

An exponential rise in price cannot be sustained. The market is bound to crash. This, of course, did occur in the coffee market. Steer clear and wait for this type of market to flatten. It may take years.

D. UPPER TRADING LEVEL: FINAL ADJUSTMENT

The lower one-third method using a 10-year monthly chart yields only a benchmark value. It certainly is not an optimum value that can be used for trading. To obtain a working upper trading level, a benchmark value will have to be adjusted to take into account current market conditions. That is, a benchmark value will have to be projected into the future to arrive at an upper trading level that is suitable for trading. There is no straightforward or mechanical way to do this. The projection requires judgment. It must integrate the current fundamental and technical factors that are currently influencing the market.

1. Use fundamental information to determine if the benchmark upper-level value should be adjusted upward (bullish) or downward (bearish).
2. Use a weekly chart to estimate the amount the upper trading level should be adjusted in the direction of the trend. Adjust the benchmark upper trading level to obtain the working value.

FIGURE 5-7

1994 December Coffee Just Prior to Its Collapse

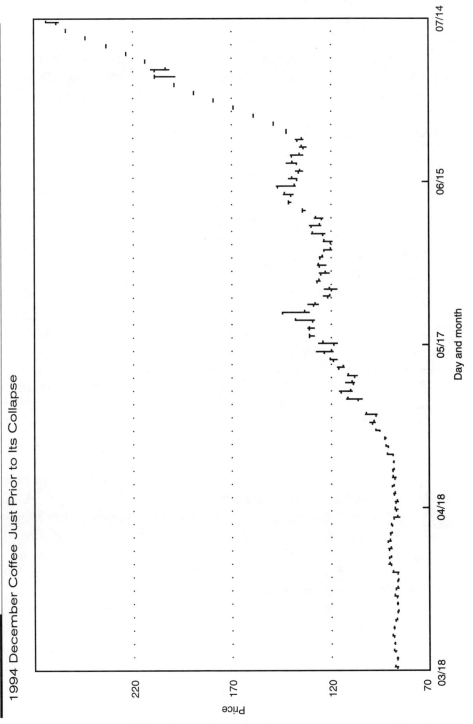

75

E. SELECTING THE INTERVAL

Interval Trading is a trade-down method. As the price erodes, contracts are purchased at predetermined lower intervals. Our analysis of drawdown and intervals leads us to the conclusion that we should make as few purchases as possible on the way down. However, we cannot take this to an extreme for two reasons:

1. We need contracts in our inventory in order to make a profit when we sell them.
2. If the interval is too wide, we will lose oscillation profits.

If we keep the interval small we will purchase too many contracts for inventory. Our drawdown can become horrendous, particularly if we misjudge the extent of the decline and set our upper trading level too high.

However, we must have contracts in inventory in order to make a profit. This fact is self-evident. However, a nagging question comes up, "Why not just buy the contracts on or near the major bottom and then sell them higher?" The answer to this question is that, if you know a major bottom is being formed, you don't need to Interval Trade. On the other hand, the closer we can start our Interval Trading program near a major bottom, the lower will be our drawdown and, thus, our risk.

Another question that comes up is, "Why not just exit your positions on the way down when you realize the market is going lower?" There are several reasons not to do this. One is that once you realize the market is going lower, it already has. If you exit your position, you are going to take a loss. The loss might appear small, but small losses add up. Another reason is that once you have exited the position, there is no hope of turning it into a profit. In addition, it seems that when you have just lost all hope that the market will ever go up, it does.

Once we have started an Interval Trading program we, for the most part, are better off to continue to Interval Trade rather than try to second-guess the market. Select a reasonable upper trading level. Buy contracts using a rather wide interval. Stick with the program.

The next question that comes up is, "What is a rather large interval?" Let's discuss this question using an example. Consider

FIGURE 5–8

The Drawdown of a V-Bottom Market

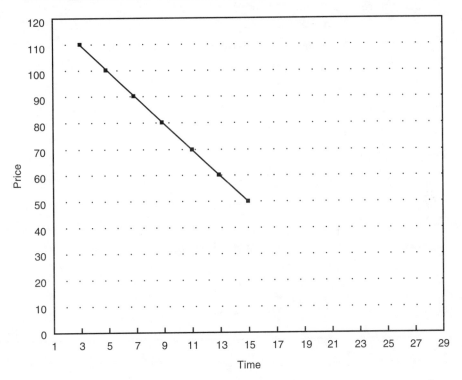

the downtrend of a hypothetical V-bottom market (Figure 5–8). For this example, we are going to assume that one point equals $50 and the initial margin is $1,000.

First, let's see what happens when we Interval Trade a market using a rather narrow 10-point interval. We will set the upper trading level at 110. The Interval Trading table is given in Table 5–2.

When the price has reached 50, our drawdown is 150 points, and we will have a total of six contracts, including the contract purchased at 50. Since each point is worth $50 and the initial margin is $1,000, our drawdown is $13,500. Each additional 10-point drop would increase our drawdown by $3,000.

Now let us see what happens when we widen the interval to 20 points. The Interval Trading table for a 20-point interval is given in Table 5–3.

TABLE 5-2

Interval Trading Table for Figure 5–8
(Upper Trading Level, 110; Interval, 10 Points)

Purchase at	Offset at	Profit Target
100	110	10
90	100	10
80	90	10
70	80	10
60	70	10
50	60	10
		Potential profit: 60 points

TABLE 5-3

Interval Table for Figure 5–8
(Upper Trading Level, 110; Interval, 20 Points)

Purchase at	Offset at	Profit Target
90	110	20
70	90	20
50	70	20
		Potential profit: 60 points

With a 20-point interval, when prices have reached 50 the total drawdown is 60 points. You would have accumulated only three contracts. The drawdown is only $6,000. If we exclude the possibility of oscillation profits, the profit potential is the same as with the previous 10-point interval. (This is not generally true. In real markets, the profit also decreases with increasing size of the interval. By doubling the size of the interval, our potential profit (excluding oscillation profits) has not been affected, but our capital requirements (therefore our risk) have been decreased by 55 percent.

If doubling the size of the interval decreases the drawdown, what happens if the interval is widened even more? With a larger interval, three things occur:

1. The price of our first interval purchase is lowered.
2. We accumulate fewer contracts in inventory.
3. Our drawdown is diminished.

FIGURE 5-9

Average Drawdown versus Interval Size, July Wheat 1983–1993

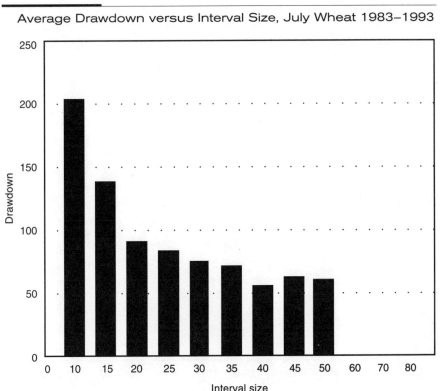

Widening the interval is advantageous in that drawdown is decreased while potential profit remains unaffected. However, two bad things occur:

1. The initial purchase price becomes lowered to the point that we might not get our first purchase.
2. The wide interval will result in the loss of oscillation profits.

A strategy to overcome these two disadvantages, the sell-buy strategy, will be discussed in Chapter 7.

Let's turn from a theoretical V-bottom market to real, but historical, markets and see what happens when the interval is increased. Figure 5–9 contains a plot of the average drawdown versus interval size for 10 years of Interval-Traded July wheat. As you can see, drawdown drops off exponentially as the interval size is increased. The curve begins to flatten at an interval size of

FIGURE 5–10

Profit versus Interval Size, July Wheat 1983–1993

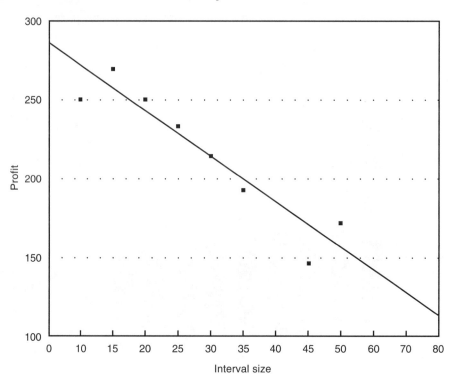

about 25 points. This analysis used the sell-buy strategy explained in Chapter 7. Therefore, a 25-point interval means that in a descending market an interval of 25 points was used, and in an ascending market an interval of 12 1/2 points was used.

Unfortunately, profits also decrease with an increasing interval (see Figure 5–10). The relationship, however, is approximately linear, as opposed to the drawdown dropoff, which was exponential. Potential profit drops off as the interval size increases. But potential drawdown drops faster.

Risk-Basis Intervals

Another approach to selecting an interval, and perhaps a more intuitively satisfying approach, is to use a value that is twice the average of the weekly high-low range. The difference between a week's high and low reflects the volatility of the market. Soy-beans are considerably more volatile than oats. Pork bellies are more volatile than live hogs.

With the aid of a computer, the average difference between the weekly high and low was obtained by using the last 10 years and the last 5 years of weekly prices. Most of the commodities recommended for Interval Trading in Table 1–1 were evaluated (see Table 5–4). A recommended interval for a sell-buy strategy is also given in the table.

T A B L E 5–4

Average Weekly Range for Selected Commodities*

Commodity	Averages		Recommended Interval†
	10-Year	5-Year	
Grains and Oilseeds			
Wheat	12.8	13.5	25
Corn	9.0	9.2	18
Oats	8.6	9.7	18
Soybeans	25.4	24.6	50
Soybean oil	1.1	0.9	2
Soybean meal	7.7	8.0	16
Livestock and Meat			
Live cattle	1.9	1.8	4
Feeder cattle	1.9	1.8	4
Live hogs	2.1	2.0	4
Pork bellies	3.8	3.7	7
Energy Complex			
Crude oil	1.1	1.1	2
Heating oil	34	33	60
Unleaded gasoline	34	34	60
Natural gas‡	—	—	—
Metals			
Gold (Comex)	11.9	10.2	20
Silver (Comex)	35.4	27.3	60
Platinum	20.9	20.1	40
Palladium	6.3	5.5	11
Copper	3.7#	4.1	8
Food and Fibers			
Cocoa	86	70	140
Coffee	6.2	5.2	10
Orange juice	4.2	4.9	10
Sugar 11	0.9	0.6	1
Cotton	2.3	2.5	5
Lumber	10.1	10.2	20

*The monthly contract with the highest open interest was used for input data.
†The recommended interval for the sell-buy strategy.
‡Insufficient data to provide meaningful ranges.
#Only seven years of data.

CHAPTER 6

Rollovers

You will not always be able to offset all of your long positions for a profit by the time the contract expires. We will refer to these losing contracts as *rollovers*. The term *rollover* is also used to mean the act of purchasing a new contract in a more distant month in order to recover a loss. Unfortunately, the term *rollover* is also applied to the new contract that is purchased. Which meaning is intended by an author must be derived from context. This chapter will discuss the strategy you should employ in handling rollovers (the losers). Later in this chapter we will discuss how to rollover (attempt to recover a rollover loss) and when to take a rollover profit (when to sell the new contract).

A. AN EXAMPLE OF ROLLOVERS

Let us begin with a specific example to define the terms and problems you will encounter. Assume that you Interval Traded 1993 July corn (Figure 6–1) using an upper trading level of 245 and an interval amount of 7 1/2 points. The Interval table for these trades is given in Table 6–1. The example is not intended to represent real Interval Trading, although it could have been actually carried out as shown. The year of the contract, its starting and ending dates, the upper trading level, and the interval in this example have been chosen so that all rollover strategies and calculations could be discussed using one example.

FIGURE 6-1

1993 July Corn Interval Trades for Rollover Example

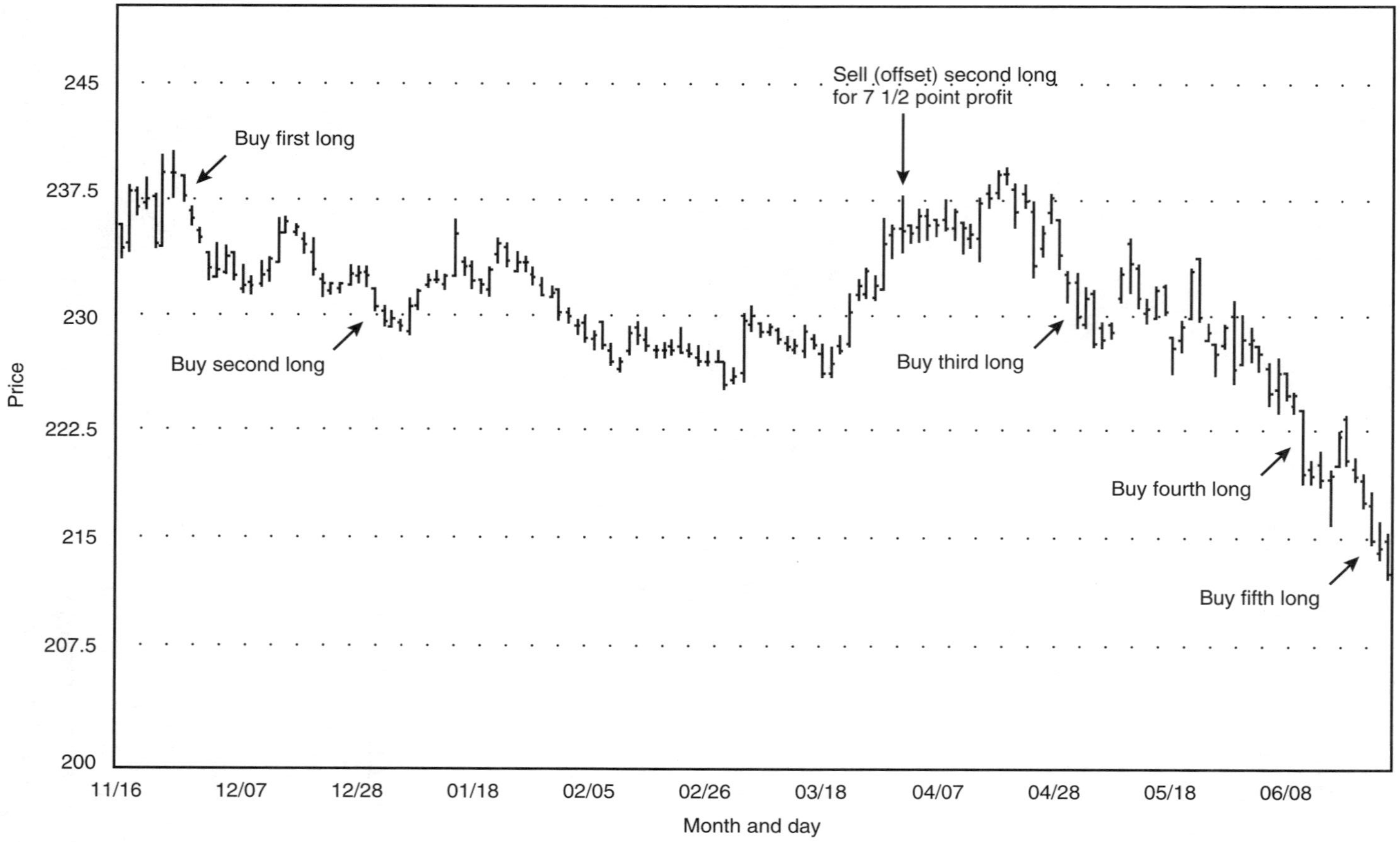

TABLE 6-1

Trading Table for 1993 July Corn
(Upper Trading Level, 345; Interval, 7 1/2)

Purchase Long at	Sell Offset at	Profit Target
237 1/2	245	7 1/2
230	237 1/2	7 1/2
222 1/2	230	7 1/2
215	222 1/2	7 1/2
207 1/2	215	7 1/2

TABLE 6-2

Trading Summary for 1993 July Corn

Date Purchased	Price Purchased	Date of Offset	Price of Offset	Profit <loss>
11/24/92	237 1/2	—	—	—
12/20/92	230	3/25/93	237 1/2	7 1/2
4/23/93	230	—	—	—
6/1/93	222 1/2	—	—	—
6/11/93	215	—	—	—

Let's assume you started trading on 11/24/92 and took your first long purchase on the low of that day at 237 1/2. In this market you would have made the trades listed in Table 6–2.

As you approach the end of the contract life (July 1993), the first decision you must make is when to offset all of your positions. Since you are holding long contracts, you will have to offset your positions before the First Notice Day in order to avoid delivery. The First Notice Day is the first day a holder of a short position can inform the Exchange of his or her intentions to deliver the physical commodity.

Delivery is made at the convenience of the seller, not the buyer. We are buyers. Therefore, we cannot select the specific date of delivery, only the seller of a contract can do that. Delivery can be made at any time on the First Notice Day or thereafter to the last day of trading. The clearinghouse (the organization that matches longs against shorts for delivery) accepts the delivery notice from the seller and assigns it to the oldest long. As Interval

T A B L E 6–3

Summary of Rollover Losses for 1993 July Corn

Date of Purchase	Price of Purchase	Offset Price*	Profit <loss>
11/24/92	237 1/2	214 1/2	<23>
4/23/93	230	214 1/2	<15 1/2>
6/1/93	222 1/2	214 1/2	<8>
6/11/93	215	214 1/2	<1/2>
		Total:	<47>

*The price at the close on 6/14/93

Traders, we have an old long (the 11/24/92 position). Consequently, on First Notice Day we have the potential of a serious financial embarrassment. Therefore, we must offset all of our long positions prior to First Notice Day. For the Chicago Board of Trade, First Notice Day is the last business day of the month preceding the delivery month. This means that for a July contract, the First Notice Day is at the end of June. In our example, we chose to offset the open contracts at the close on 6/14/93 at 214 1/2, the price of the close several days in advance of First Notice Day.

Because of impending delivery, we are forced to offset all four of our positions at a loss. The losses that occurred by the forced exit are called *rollover losses*. (See Table 6–3.) These losses are real losses. No amount of bookkeeping gimmickry can convert them into a profit. We must enter them on our tally sheet as a loss. The fact that we plan to recover the losses in the future by a rollover must not be construed to mean they are not losses.

B. HOW TO HANDLE ROLLOVERS

Using this example, let us look at the strategies to handle rollover losses.

Don't Take a New Position in an Old Contract

Why take a position that we know will generate a rollover loss? When the 11/24/92 position was entered, we had no idea that it

might generate a rollover loss. In fact, chances were fairly good
that it would not. However, this is not true of the 6/11/93 position.
We should have never taken this position. At that point in time
(6/11/93), we would have known that we were trading in a rather
weak market. We would have also known that we would have to
exit the position in just a few days. In the weak market, the possibility of the market rallying to provide a 7 1/2 point profit in just
a few days is rather slim. Don't take a new position in an old contract. Use a more distant month for the new position. The idea
here is to avoid taking a position you know you will have to
rollover in the near future. Take the position in a more distant
month and avoid the rollover.

Start looking at the more distant contracts one to two
months in advance of the First Notice Day to see if you can take a
new position in the deferred contract. Be sure to check if the new
position in the more distant contract would be in the same crop
year or in a new crop year. If it is in the same crop year, then the
fundamentals that apply to the old contract will also apply to the
new one. The July contract in corn is the last contract of the crop
year. Therefore, the rollover contract in a more distant month will
have to be in the new crop year. Supply and demand factors can
be expected to be quite different.

Accept a Small Loss Rather than Rollover
The next principle is to take small losses at rollover time. Let's
assume you did take the 6/11/93 position. Your rollover loss is 1/2
point or $25.00 (plus commissions, of course). Just accept this loss
as part of doing business in commodities. Ignore it and begin to
Interval Trade in the more distance month.

In fact, we suggest that you write off anything that is less
than about one-half of your interval. With a 7 1/2 point interval,
write off losses of 3 1/4 points or less. With a 20-point interval, accept any rollover loss up to about 10 points.

Don't be stubborn about rollover losses or compulsive about
trying to recover all of them. Each new position you take has its
own risk of drawdown and its own potential for a rollover loss. The
added risk of taking a position just to recover a small rollover loss is
not worth it. With the proper strategy, you will find interval Trading

will produce a profit even if you don't roll over any contracts. However, your profit will be vastly improved if you do use rollovers.

C. OVERVIEW OF ROLLOVER STRATEGY

If we don't want to write off our loss, then we will have to try to recover it with a new contract or contracts in a distant month of the commodity. Our discussion here deals with the purchase of a new contract in a more distant month to recover a rollover loss.

The first goal of a rollover is to avoid another rollover loss. The second goal is to recover your old rollover loss and, if possible, the profit you should have been able to make in the old contract.

There are two general techniques for rolling over into a more distant contract. Neither method works all the time, and, unfortunately, it is not predictable which should be used or avoided. Judgment is required. These techniques are:

1. An immediate rollover.
2. A deferred rollover.

In an *immediate rollover,* we purchase the new long positions in the deferred month at the same time we terminate our old long positions. In a *deferred rollover,* as the name implies, we defer entering the distant month.

Before discussing these two basic strategies to recover a rollover loss, we should point out there is a third rollover strategy—the *anticipated rollover.* You use an anticipated rollover to enter a more distant contract when your current contract *has a profit* and is about to expire. In this case, you would buy the more distant contract before you sell the current contract. Therefore, you would be holding two contracts of the same commodity, but in two different contract months. Plan to offset the current contract on any market weakness. Also make a new interval table for the new contract based upon your entry price.

D. AN IMMEDIATE ROLLOVER OF A SINGLE CONTRACT

In an immediate rollover, we purchase a new long position at the same time we exit our old one. Assume we want to rollover only one of the contracts of the 1993 July corn. For example, suppose we choose to roll over the 23-point loss we incurred in the 11/24/92 trade. In an immediate rollover, we would purchase our new long contract, the rollover contract, in the 1993 December corn also at the close on 6/14/93. The close of December corn on 6/14/93 was 227 (see Figure 6–2). (The closes are used in this example only because they are at specific prices that occurred at the same time on 6/14/93. In the real world, you would have carried out the transactions during the day. In looking back on the historical data for this day, we cannot say what the exact prices would have been at the same time during the day; hence, we use the closes for our example and its calculations.)

This new purchase is not part of our Interval Trading program for the December contract. We also might have decided to interval trade the December 1993 corn independent of this additional purchase. The two are unrelated except for their combined drawdown of our account.

Offset of the Rollover

Once we are in this new position, the rollover position, we have to decide where to exit. Our rollover loss in the 11/24/92 position of the July contract, the one we are rolling over, is 23 points. We have two choices. In the first choice, we can set a target price in the December corn contract 23 points above our purchase. Our entry price, the close in the 1993 December corn contract on 6/14/93, was 227. The target offsetting price would be 250. This value is calculated by adding the rollover loss to the closing price. In this choice, we would only recover our capital. We would not also attempt to recover our hoped-for profit.

Rollover loss:	23
December corn 6/14 close:	<u>227</u>
Target price without profit (sum):	250

In the second choice, we would also try to get the hoped-for profit as well as the lost capital. In this choice we would add our rollover loss (23 points) and the desired profit (7 1/2 points) to the close (227) to get the offset price (257 1/2). What you do depends

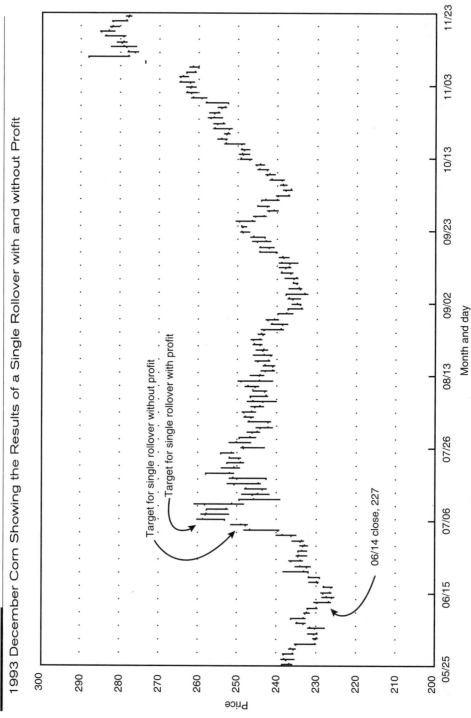

FIGURE 6-2

1993 December Corn Showing the Results of a Single Rollover with and without Profit

Target for single rollover without profit

Target for single rollover with profit

06/14 close, 227

Month and day

Price

upon your view of the commodity and the likelihood of a major move.

Rollover loss:	23
December corn 6/14 close:	227
Desired profit:	7 1/2
Target price with profit (sum):	257 1/2

Regardless of which choice you use, the rollover contract is not Interval Traded. If the price should drop by 7 1/2 points, we do not buy another contract. This contract is strictly for recovering rollover loss and, if you are so inclined, the hoped-for profit.

The offset targets are marked on the December corn chart in Figure 6–2.

What happens if the price continues to drop? You have one of two choices to make, both unpleasant—liquidate or hold. If you think you are in the start of an intermediate or major bear market, you probably should liquidate your position. Re-establish your long position at a lower price at some time in the future. Use your combined losses to determine your target price.

Alternatively, you can hold your position, ride it down, and roll it over if necessary. If you decide on this latter strategy, be sure you have sufficient capital to see it through for a potentially extended period of time.

E. AN IMMEDIATE ROLLOVER OF MULTIPLE CONTRACTS

Let's take a slightly more complex case to see how we handle multiple contracts purchased at different prices. Let's rollover all four contracts of 1993 July corn. The sum of the roll over losses you would have incurred on 6/14/93 is 47 points (see Table 6–3).

The rollovers into the new contract involve a modified averaging-down strategy (see Chapter 2). The calculations are as follows:

1. *Calculate your average rollover loss.*

Contract	Rollover Loss
1	23
2	15 1/2
3	8
4	1/2
Total:	47

Average = (47)/4 = 11 3/4 points

2. *Calculate your rollover target value.*
Once you have your average rollover loss, you can calculate your rollover target value. You can use two values: one that includes the profit you should have made and one that does not include that "profit."

Rollover Target without "Profit"
Our goal in this case is to get our capital back and forget any profit we should have had. This is a conservative goal and should be used if you feel the market you are about to roll into is weak. The target price is just the average value.

Average rollover loss:	11 3/4
December corn 6/14 close:	227
Target price without profit (sum):	238 3/4

The target offsets are marked on the December corn chart in Figure 6–3.

Rollover Target Value with "Profit"
Our goal in this case is to make the money we should have made in the last Interval Trade. We were using a 7 1/2-point interval. Therefore, we add 7 1/2 points to the average value.

Average rollover loss:	11 3/4
December corn 6/14 close:	227
Desired profit:	7 1/2
Target price with profit (sum):	238 3/4

The calculation involves adding the interval value to the average rollover loss. If the interval had been 20 points, then we would have added 20 points to the average rollover loss.

In our example, the target price (with profit) is 238 3/4 points. What we must offset are four contracts at 238 3/4 or 20 1/2 points higher than our purchase price in the new contract (the 1993 December contract in our example). The value "four," the rollover number, arises from the fact that we had four contracts to rollover. Had we incurred a rollover loss with five contracts, then the rollover number would have been five.

FIGURE 6-3

December 1993 Corn Showing the Results of Rolling Over Multiple Contracts

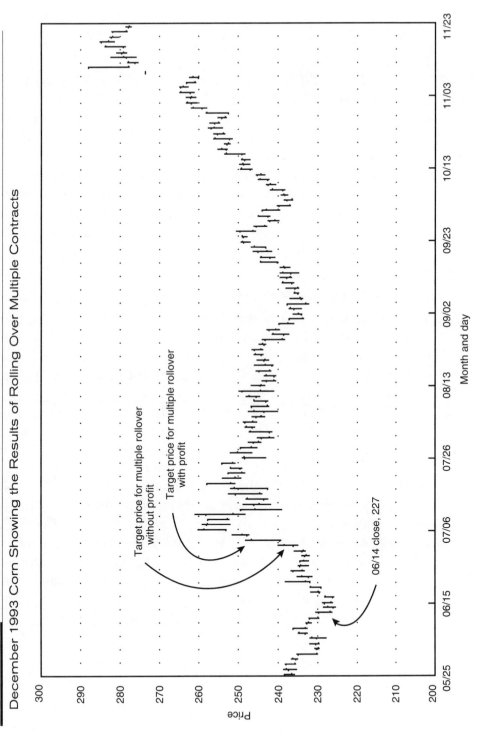

93

The target offsets are marked on the December corn chart in Figure 6–3.

The above example was selected with historical hindsight to explain the calculations used for rollovers. As with any futures contract, there is no guarantee you will be able to make your target price.

What should you do if you don't make your target price? When you offset your rollovers in the new month, calculate a new average value using all rollover losses and profits from the original and new contracts. Armed with this new average, make the decision whether you want to roll over again. Each case will be different and judgment will be required.

F. DEFERRED ROLLOVERS

The idea behind a deferred rollover is to hold off taking the new position until conditions are favorable for a price rise. Unfortunately, there is no surefire way of knowing when this is the case. Judgment, as well as the ability to carry out technical and fundamental analysis, is required.

The calculations for the deferred rollover are the same as for the immediate rollover. The average loss is calculated. A decision is made as to whether you wish to recover the lost capital plus the profit you should have made, or just the lost capital. The rollover target value is then calculated. Once the position is taken, the rollover target value is added to the entry price to get the target price.

One straightforward technique that avoids the need to determine an adequate entry point is to double up on new interval positions. At each main-buy point, buy two (rather than one) contracts. Offset one of the positions at the standard interval level and offset the other at the rollover target price.

CHAPTER 7

The Sell-Buy:
More Profits at Lower Risk

In Chapter 5 we saw that, by expanding the interval, we solved two problems. We can diminish our drawdown and accumulate fewer contracts during the downtrend phase of the market cycle. With fewer accumulated contracts, we would expect to have a smaller drawdown and fewer rollover losses when things go awry. A large interval, however, is not a cure-all. With a large interval, we could also miss many oscillation profits.

When commodity prices approach a major bottom, they generally form some type of pattern other than the V-bottom we have been using as an example. A typical pattern would be a classical inverted head-and-shoulders pattern, a type of bottom oscillation (see Figure 7–1). Another type of pattern would be a flutter, where prices move, for the most part, sideways and oscillate.

These oscillations are a disaster for trend traders, but can be golden for Interval Traders, provided, of course, your interval is small enough to catch the oscillations. For example, in Figure 7–2, with an interval of 10 points, all of the oscillations would be captured as oscillation trades. With an interval of 20 points and purchases at 70 and 50, however, you would have missed all of them.

We must reduce our drawdown by increasing our interval size, yet we do not want to increase the interval size to the point that we will miss the oscillation profits. This chapter presents one technique to partly resolve this dilemma: a sell-buy at an intermediate level.

FIGURE 7-1

Line Drawing of an Inverted Head-and-Shoulders Bottom

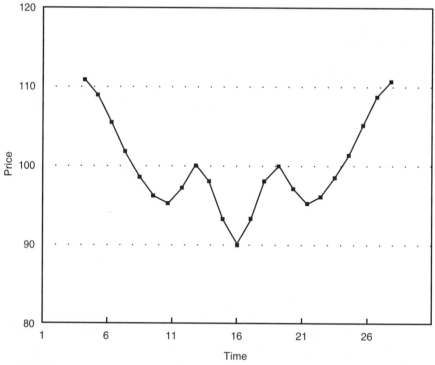

FIGURE 7-2

A Downtrend in a Market with an Exaggerated Bottom Oscillation

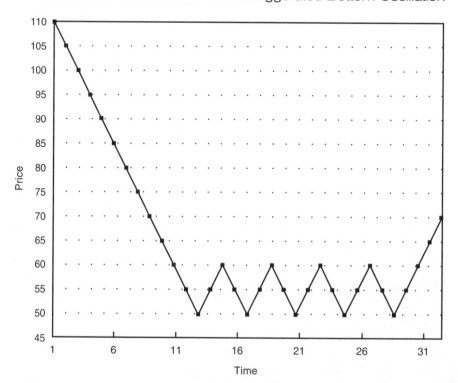

FIGURE 7–3

Using a Variable Interval

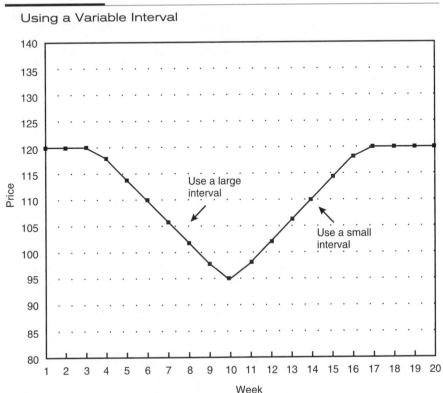

A. THE SELL-BUY STRATEGY

What we would like to do is to use a large interval during the downtrend of a cycle then switch to a small interval near the bottom and use it during the uptrend (see Figure 7–3). In the real world, this is impossible to do with accuracy because we can't identify a bottom until well after it has occurred.

However, we can approximate the ideal case by using a sell-buy strategy. So that we can discuss this strategy, let's call the buy levels that are separated by the interval amount the *main-buy levels* (or main-buy points). We will then establish *intermediate sell-buy levels* (or intermediate-buy points) that are halfway between the main-buy levels. The market in Figure 7–4 has main-buy levels at 90, 70, and 50 when the interval is set at 20 points. The intermediate sell-buy levels in this market would be at 100, 80, and 60. The expanded Interval Table for this market is shown in Table 7–1.

FIGURE 7–4

Identification of Main-Buy Levels and Intermediate Sell-Buy Levels

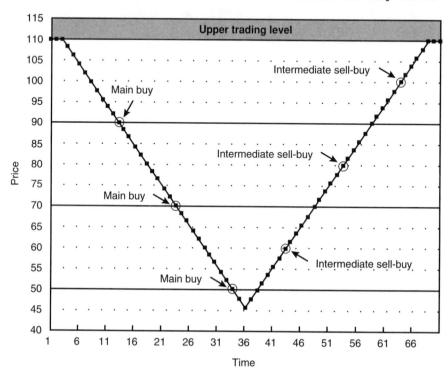

TABLE 7–1

Expanded Interval Table
(Upper Trading Level, 110; Interval, 20; Intermediate Level, 10)

Main Buy	Intermediate Sell-Buy	Offset Sale	Profit Target
—	100	110	10
90	—	100	10
—	80	90	10
70	—	80	10
—	60	70	10
50	—	60	10
			Potential profit: 60 points

F I G U R E 7–5

The Sell-Buy Technique

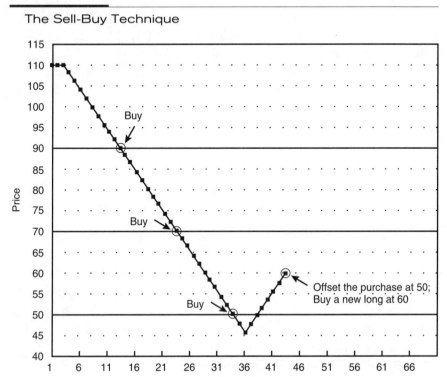

We define a sell-buy as follows:

Sell-Buy: At an intermediate level, sell a main-level contract for a profit and buy a new contract.

An intermediate sell-buy level is used if, and only if, we own, or have owned, a contract at the main level immediately below the intermediate price. For example in Figure 7–4, if we own a long contract at 50 (the main-buy level), and if the market rises to 60, we would sell the 50 position and buy a new contract at 60, the intermediate-buy level. However, if we own a long contract at 50 and the market continues down to 30 (the next lower main-buy level), we do not buy another contract at 40 (the next lower intermediate-buy level). We do not buy because we do not, nor have we recently, owned a contract at 30.

Consider the price pattern in Figure 7–5. The price has collapsed from 110 to 45 over the time period shown. During this downtrend we purchased three long positions, at 90, 70, and 50. When the price reaches 50, our drawdown is $6,000 (using $50 per point and a margin of $1,000 per contract). This is the drawdown we had anticipated with a 20-point interval.

When prices begin their rally from 50 and move to 60, we sell our 50 contract for a 10-point profit. At the same time, we purchase a new long contract at 60. We have carried out a sell-buy transaction at the intermediate level of 60. We are now long at 90, 70, and 60, but no longer have a position at 50. These transactions are shown in Figure 7–5.

B. WHY SELL THEN BUY? WHY NOT JUST HOLD?

At first blush, a sell-buy strategy sounds like churning—excessive trading solely to generate commissions for the broker. Why sell the contract and immediately buy another at approximately the same price? Why not just hold the one you have? The answer to these questions is that it is to your advantage to sell then buy, rather than just hold. Since this is not intuitively obvious and because it is controversial, let us discuss it in detail.

Our goals in Interval Trading are

1. To take profits if the market moves to a higher level.
2. To protect ourselves if the market collapses.
3. To take profits if the market oscillates.

One of the above three will occur, but we don't know which one. Our strategy must position us in the market so that we can take advantage of the first and the third, should either occur, and protect ourselves should the second case occur.

The sell-buy does indeed generate more commissions than a mere hold. However, it is the price we must pay to position ourselves in the market to achieve our goals. To see why, let us examine the three possibilities. In considering these examples, keep in mind that (1) we don't know what the future holds, and (2) if we did know, we would not be Interval Trading.

Possibility 1

Just after a sell-buy, the market goes straight up. In this case, the sell-buy is a waste of commission money. Had you known that this

FIGURE 7–6

Possibility 1: Prices Keep Rising after the Sell-Buy.
The Sell-Buy Strategy Offers No Advantage. A Commission Will
Be Wasted.

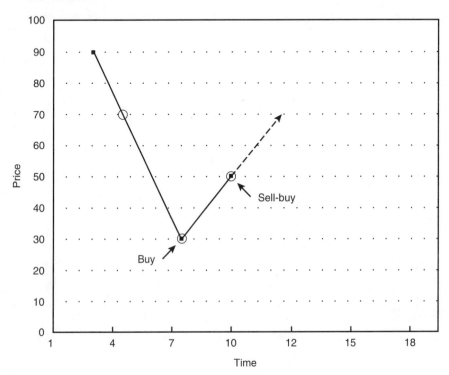

was going to happen, you would have not sold then bought. You
would have just held and saved the commission. However, because you bought after the sell, you are still in the market and
will profit by the price increase. Had you just sold, you would
have been out of the market and would have missed the price rise
and the profit you could have made on it. (See Figure 7–6.)

Possibility 2

Just after the sell-buy, the market collapses. In this case, you are
also out a commission. However, you are not any worse off than if
you had just held. The profit you realized on the sell portion of the
sell-buy will equal the drawdown to the original buy level. Again,
had you known this was going to happen, you would have sold but
not bought. (See Figure 7–7.)

FIGURE 7–7

Possibility 2: The Market Collapses after a Sell-Buy.
The Sell-Buy Strategy Offers No Advantage. A Commission Will
Be Wasted.

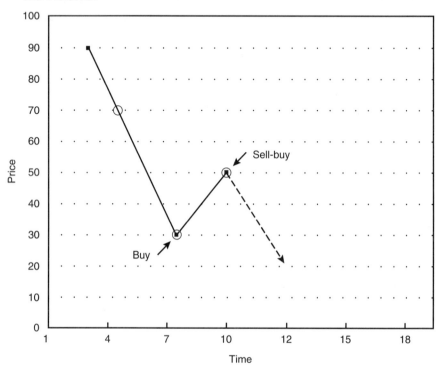

Possibility 3

Possibilities 1 and 2 are a waste of commission money. Had you
known either was going to occur, you could have saved yourself a
commission by simply holding your position. However, as the price
pattern was developing, you would not have known if either was
going to occur. This brings us to the third possibility—the market
starts to move essentially sideways with oscillations. It is in this
case that the sell-buy provides an advantage. (See Figure 7–8.)

The sell provides an oscillation profit. The profit protects
against (pays for) the price erosion back to the lower level. You
must sell, then buy. If you just sell and don't also buy, you will get
the oscillation profit but miss all further profit if the market continues to rise. If you just hold (neither buy nor sell) and the market drops back to the lower level, you will miss the oscillation

FIGURE 7-8

The Sell-Buy

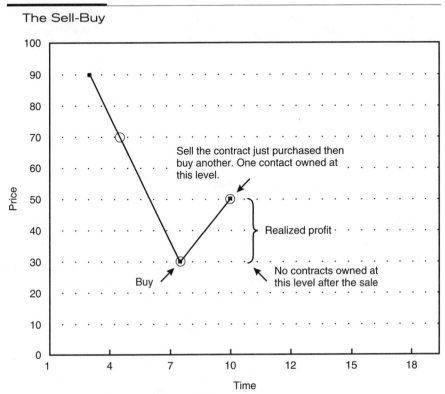

profit. Should you then buy another contract at this lower level in anticipation of another oscillation, you will accumulate contracts at this lower level without benefit of an oscillation profit.

> The Sell: (a) captures an oscillation profit;and (b) opens up the price level just below the sell-buy level so that another contract can be purchased.
>
> The Buy: Keeps us in the market, should the market keep rising.

Let's look at some exaggerated examples to explain the advantage of the sell-buy. First, consider the result of buying contracts at a lower level and not offsetting them as the market oscillates. This course of action can be illustrated using the graph in

FIGURE 7-9

One Possible Outcome of a Buy-and-Hold Strategy.
Too Many Contracts Accumulate at One Price Level; a Potentially
Large Drawdown.

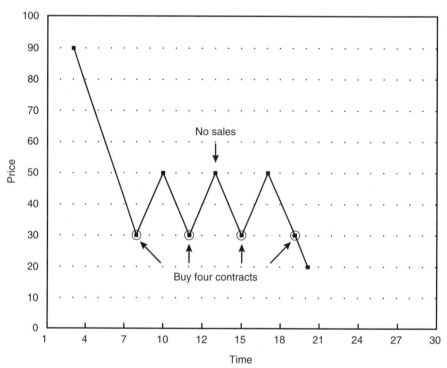

Figure 7–9. Assume we hold one contract and buy another contract each time the price falls to the lower level. Because we don't
sell any of these contracts, we have no oscillation profits, and we
will accumulate far too many contracts at the lower level. Should
the market move up, we would reap a handsome profit. However,
we can't count on that. We have to protect ourselves. Should the
market continue to move down, we would have a very large and
potentially disastrous drawdown.

Next let's assume we just buy and hold. No additional contracts at the lower price level are purchased. In this case, we
would miss all the oscillation profits. (See Figure 7–10.)

In the sell-buy strategy we sell the contract we purchased at
a lower level. Then we immediately buy it back. Two transactions

Another Possible Outcome of a Buy and Hold Strategy.
No Accumulation of Contracts and No Oscillation Profits.

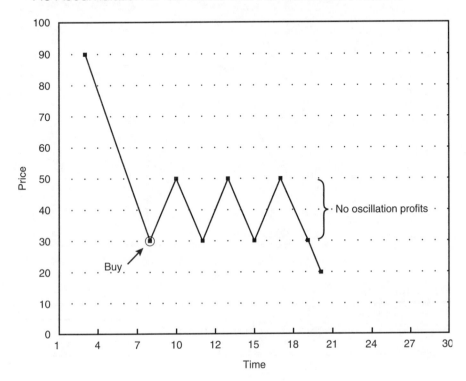

are made at the intermediate level—a sell and a buy. We now can
buy another contract at the lower level without worrying about
excessive accumulation. If the market drops lower, we don't buy
again until a much lower level. If the market rises, we take an oscillation profit and still have a contract to take advantage of any
additional market advance. (See Figure 7–11.)

To further illustrate the sell-buy strategy, consider the cir-
cled buys and their offsets in Figure 7–12. As you can see, if the
market collapses after a series of sell-buys, then we are left with
only two open contracts. However, we have captured (in the example) three oscillation profits.

Should the market advance after a series of sell-buys, we
would capture (again in the example) four oscillation profits. As

FIGURE 7–11

The Sell-Buy Strategy

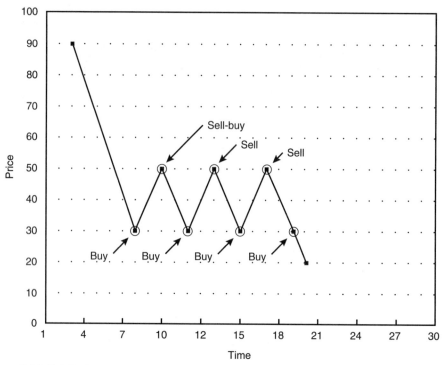

FIGURE 7–12

The Sell-Buy Strategy with Three Oscillation Profits.
Two Open Contracts Will Be Held in a Falling Market.

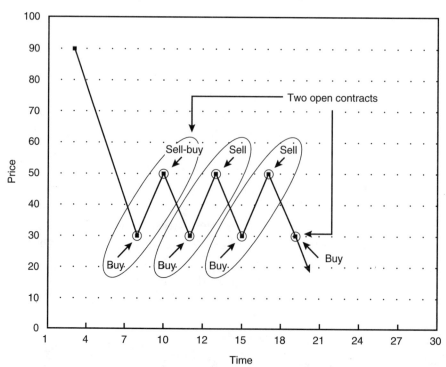

FIGURE 7-13

The Sell-Buy Strategy in a Rising Market.
Four Oscillation Profits Will Be Taken and One Open Contract Is
Held.

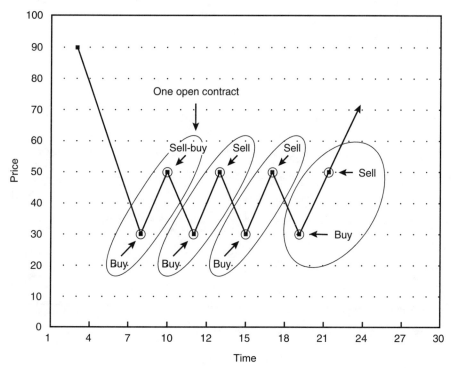

the prices advance above our intermediate level, we will still have
one open contract to capture profit during the price rise regardless of the number of oscillation profits we take at this level. (See
Figure 7–13.)

The sell-buy allows us to trade with a large interval during a
price decline so we can minimize the drawdown. When prices
begin to rise, the sell-buy allows us to automatically switch to a
smaller interval. This is the strategy we want. We want to maxi-
mize our profits (oscillation profits) and minimize our risks
(drawdown). The sell-buy also allows us to take advantage of any
sustained uptrend move by keeping us in the market.

FIGURE 7–14

Case 1. A Flat Market after the Sell-Buy

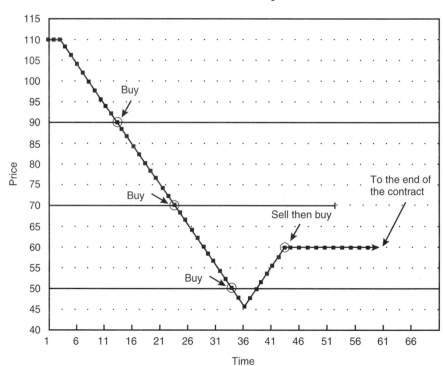

C. FURTHER CONSIDERATION OF THE SELL-BUY STRATEGY

Once we have made a sell-buy, one of three things can happen:

1. The price movement can turn flat and remain so until expiration.
2. The price movement can move down.
3. The price movement can move up.

Case 1: The Price Movement Can Turn Flat and Remain So until Expiration

It makes no difference where we are or what size interval we are using, if the market turns flat and stays that way until the contract expires, then we are going to take a rollover loss (see Figure 7–14). Depending upon the fundamental and technical evaluation

FIGURE 7-15

Case 2. A Price Drop after a Sell-Buy

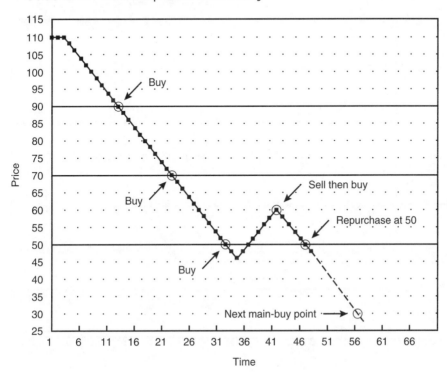

you make at this point in time, you may take a rollover position to recover your loss, or you may decide to use your capital elsewhere.

Case 2: Prices Move Down

If the prices continue downward, then they will cross (in our example) the 50 main-buy point. Therefore, we will add a new contract to inventory. In Figure 7–15 this means we would have four long contracts: 90, 70, 60, and 50. Our next level of purchase will be at the main-buy point at 30 (20 points lower), and not at the intermediate-buy point of 40 (10 points lower).

This strategy allows us to return to a large interval as the market drops. Thus we minimize the number of contracts we accumulate. With fewer contracts, our drawdown is less and our potential rollover loss is less. Therefore, our risk is less. This is our goal.

F I G U R E 7–16

Case 3. Prices Continue Upward after a Sell-Buy

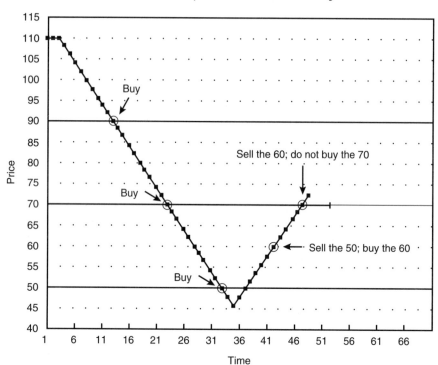

Case 3: The Price Movement Can Move Up

If, after our sell-buy, the price continues upward (in our example) to 70, then we will sell the contract we had purchased at the intermediate level of 60. However, 70 is a main-buy point, and we already own a contract at this level. Therefore, we do not purchase another contract at 70. It is not a sell-buy point (see Figure 7–16).

What happens after a sell at 70? If the market turns flat or if it continues upward, the answer should be fairly obvious. We can't do anything in a flat market. We will sell-buy at the next intermediate point (80).

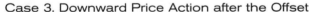

FIGURE 7–17

Case 3. Downward Price Action after the Offset

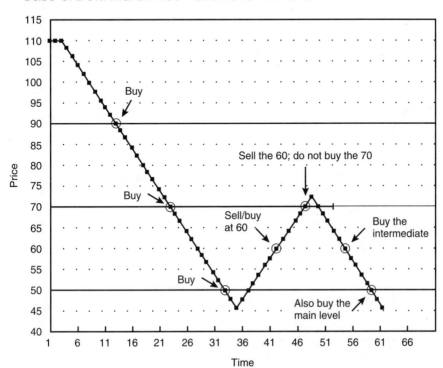

However, a problem does arise if the market should turn down after our 70 sell. Where do we repurchase a new long? At 60 (10 points down) or at 50 (20 points down)? Another possibility is to purchase at both 60 and 50. All cases are logical. What you should do at this point depends on your capital and your outlook for the market. If your evaluation of the market is bullish, then you should take both positions. If your outlook is neutral or bearish, then you should only make a purchase at the lower main-buy level (at 50 points in our example).

FIGURE 7-18

Buy at the Main-Buy Levels

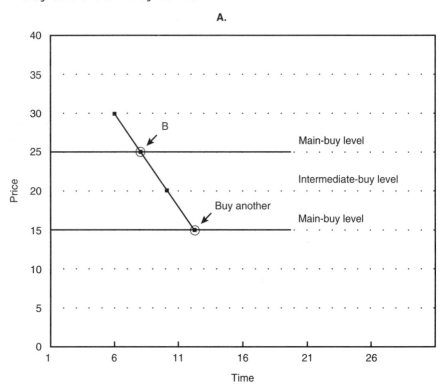

D. SUMMARY OF THE SELL-BUY SYSTEM OF INTERVAL TRADING

The rules for the sell-buy strategy and for Interval Trading can be summarized as follows (B = buy a long contract; S/B = sell then immediately buy a contract; S = sell a contract).

Falling Market:
    1. Always buy at the main levels. (See Figure 7–18.)

FIGURE 7–18

Continued

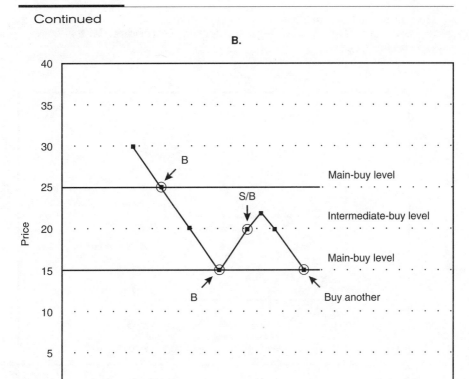

FIGURE 7-19

Buy at the Intermediate
(If You Have Owned and Sold a Contract Purchased at the Main-
Buy Level below It)

A.

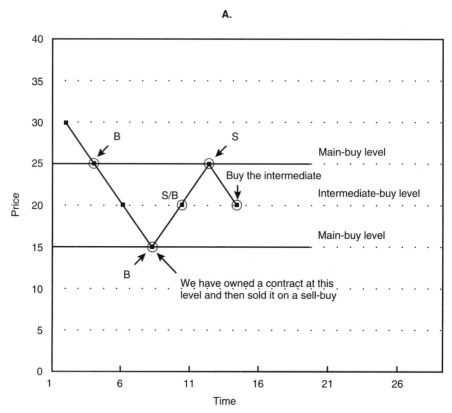

2. Buy at an intermediate level if, and only if, we have
owned and sold a contract at the main level just below the
intermediate level. (See Figure 7–19.)

FIGURE 7–19

Continued

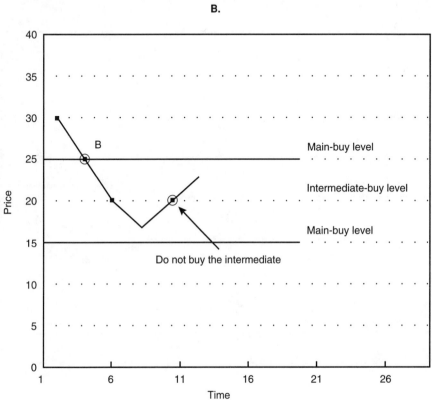

B.

FIGURE 7–19

Continued

C.

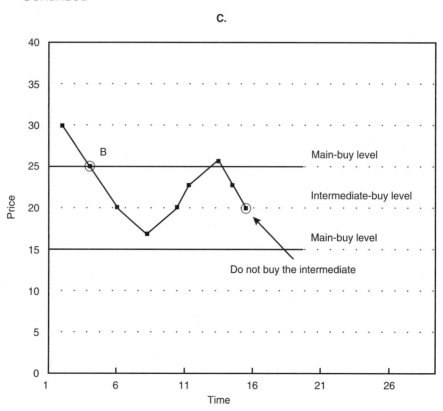

FIGURE 7–20

Sell-Buy at the Intermediate
(If You Own a Contract at the Main-Buy Level Just below It)

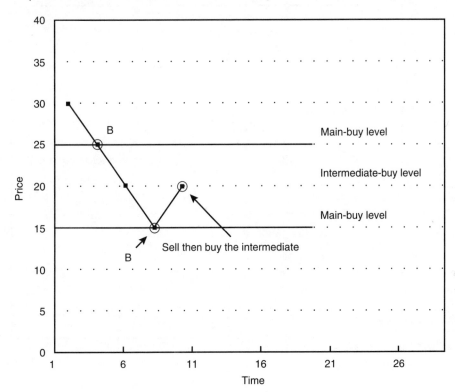

Rising Market:

   1. Sell-buy at the intermediate levels if you own a contract
   at the main level just below the intermediate level. (See
   Figure 7–20.)

FIGURE 7–21

Sell Only at a Main-Buy Level

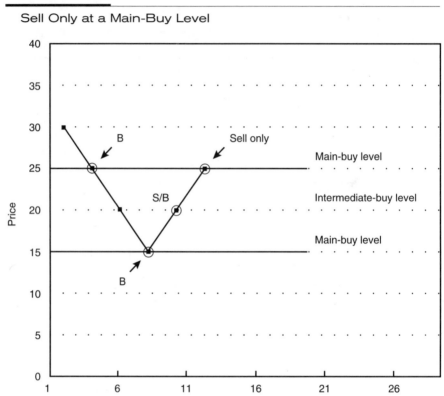

2. Sell only (do not buy) at the main level if you own a
   contract at that level. (See Figure 7–21.)

FIGURE 7-22

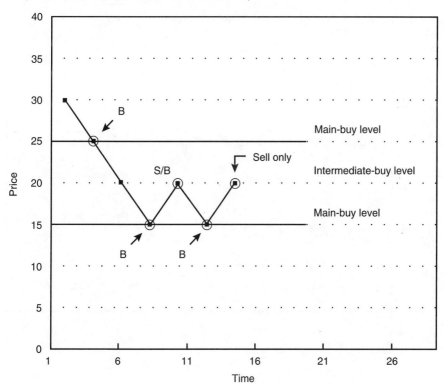

Sell Only at an Intermediate Level
(If You Own a Contract at That Level)

3. Sell only (do not buy) at an intermediate level if you own a contract at that level. (See Figure 7–22.)

FIGURE 7–23

Sell-Buy at the Main Level
(If You Do Not Own a Contract at That Level)

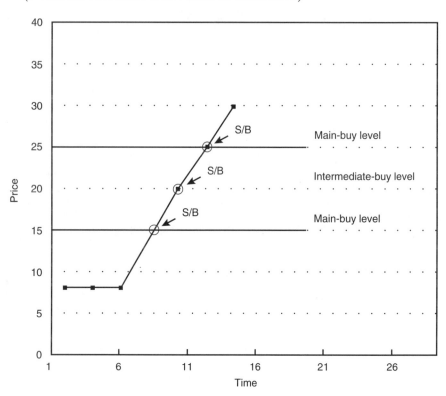

4. Sell-buy at the main level if you don't own a contract at that level. (See Figure 7–23.)

5. Sell only (do not buy) at the upper trading level, or switch to a trend-following strategy.

E. PRACTICAL ASPECTS OF INTERVAL TRADING

In Interval Trading, place your orders with your broker well in advance of their potential execution. Do not wait for the prices to cross a main- or intermediate-buy level before taking action. One of the advantages of Interval Trading is that you know in advance what you want to do and where you want to do it. By placing these orders with the broker before they can be executed, they will remain as open orders (good until cancelled). Should the market touch them during the day (on a price run, for example) they will be executed automatically. This frees you of the need to continually watch the market during the day. Once-a-day inspection after the markets have closed will be all you need for Interval Trading.

Don't Sell Then Buy at the Same Price

Because of the mechanics of how trading actually takes place, don't enter your sell and buy orders at exactly the same price. What could happen is that the buy can be executed but the sell remain unfilled and be followed by a market collapse. The result is that you would be long two positions with no oscillation profits. To avoid this possibility, place your sell order one or two ticks below your buy order. In this way, your sell order must be executed before the market can touch and activate your buy order. Although it is rather rare, it is extremely profitable to have your sell order executed and your buy unfilled followed by a market collapse. In such a case, you purchase the missed contract at a lower price and do not have the burden of the drawdown from a higher-priced purchase. Therefore, whenever possible, straddle an even number, such as 250 or 300, with a sell and buy. There is a propensity for commodity prices to stop at even numbers and reverse their direction. Place the sell just below the even number and the buy just above. In the grains, for example, if you plan to sell and buy at 300, place your sell at 299 1/2 and your buy at 300 1/2 (stop). (Your order must be entered as a "stop order", otherwise the floor broker will probably execute the trade at a lower price.)

CHAPTER 8

What Can Go Wrong

Don't be so naive as to think that you can't lost money by Interval Trading. It can happen in a number of ways. In this chapter, we will look at the usual ways you can lose money. Undoubtedly, new ways will be discovered in the future.

A. HOW YOU CAN LOSE MONEY IN INTERVAL TRADING

In general, you will lose money because of your own actions or because of an unpredictable market action.

Your Own Actions

You can lose money by not understanding how Interval Trading works or by being overly optimistic about the bullish potential of the market. For example, you may

1. Start to Interval Trade at too high a price.
2. Purchase only a few contracts near a major top.
3. Use an interval that is too small.
4. Make imprudent rollovers.
5. Start to Interval Trade with insufficient capital.

Particularly insidious is a combination of these errors: for example, purchasing contracts that are too close together at a relatively high price, using an underfunded account. Given these circumstances, you would be lucky to get out with the shirt on your back.

Unpredictable Market Action

While errors listed above are under your control, and thus avoidable, there are circumstances not under your control that also will cause you to lose money. These include

1. The market, after you begin to Interval Trade, goes almost straight down.
2. The market, again after you have begun to Interval Trade, becomes inactive (flat) and remains that way for an extended period of time (maybe years).

The combination of these two types—a market going straight down and then turning flat for an extended period of time—is guaranteed to be a loser. Given these circumstances, "You Can't Win Trading Commodities."

Regardless of the cause—your error, a nasty market, or a combination of the two—what actually occurs is that your drawdown becomes excessive and you are forced to liquidate contracts at a great financial loss in order to maintain liquidity.

In Interval Trading, you must do four things to avoid a financial disaster:

1. Be well informed.
2. Diversify your holdings.
3. Use a large interval.
4. Don't overtrade your capital.

Be Informed   To make money in Interval Trading, you have to know what you are doing. You must understand how Interval Trading works and you must know your potential drawdown. You must also know the relationship between interval and drawdown. You must know how to calculate drawdown and select upper trading levels. Only knowledge will save you from yourself.

You cannot ignore the fundamental and technical aspects of the market. You must know the basic features that control the supply and demand of the commodity. You must also know about seasonal trends. These are the fundamentals. You can't ignore technical factors either. Is the monthly trend up? What about the weekly? Where is the major support and resistance? What about the cycle tops and bottoms? This book has been restricted to just a discussion of the mechanics of Interval Trading. However, fundamental and technical factors are needed to adjust the benchmark upper trading level to a working level that you will use for actual trading.

Diversify   Don't put all your cookies in one jar. Don't buy two contracts of the same commodity. Buy one contract in two different commodities. Only diversification will save you from the unexpected. The mechanics of diversification are discussed in Chapter 11.

Diversification has been sound advice for investors since investing began. Diversification is also sound advice for the intelligent commodity speculator. Interval Trade as many different and different types of commodities as your capital will allow. Use large intervals in all of them so that you will not become deeply committed to any one commodity. The chances that all the commodities you are trading will turn ugly at the same time are remote. While one or two of your commodities may be doing poorly, the others will be generating oscillation profits.

However, a meltdown of the entire commodity sector is not impossible. Keep your eye on the Commodity Research Bureau Index (CRB, the commodity equivalent of the S&P or Dow Jones indexes). If it goes into a major downtrend, you may have to adjust your portfolio.

You can make a killing by risking all your capital on one Interval Trade, but that is not intelligent speculation. Our goal is to make a high percentage return on our capital, not a killing.

Use a Large Interval   We have discussed the reasons for using a large interval in some detail in previous chapters. Using a large interval is a risk-reducing tactic. Should the market turn against you, a large interval prevents you from accumulating too many contracts. Coupled with the sell-buy strategy, the large interval provides a relatively low-risk strategy suitable for intelligent commodity speculation.

Don't Overtrade your Capital   To be successful, you have to match your capital against your potential drawdown. If you take positions in too many commodities, the potential exists for an excessive drawdown in one or more, forcing you to liquidate at a great loss. Interval Trading will be successful if, and only if, you protect yourself against excessive drawdown.

B. DON'T START INTERVAL TRADING AT TOO HIGH A PRICE

It is extremely tempting, after watching a commodity price drop for a number of months, to say to yourself, "It can't go much lower. Let's start Interval Trading it now!" However, to be on the safe side, start Interval Trading only in the lower one-third of the 10-year price range.

The principal problem with starting Interval Trading too high is that you won't be able to offset your uppermost contracts before rollover time. The entire period of time you hold these contracts, your account will be depressed by their drawdown. If you try to unload them early, you will, of course, take a real loss. If you hold them to rollover time, you will have to take a rollover loss (which is also a real loss).

Before you jump into an Interval Trade, calculate the potential drawdown from the current price to its 10-year low, perhaps even to its 20-year low. Ask yourself, "Am I willing to risk that amount of money just to start Interval Trading now?" Calculate the upper trading level. Check the fundamental and technical reports before you begin. Make sure the seasonal trend is in your favor. In some circumstances it is all right to start higher than the recommended lower one-third. Just be careful and be sure you are well informed. Commodities have the knack of doing the unexpected.

Once you have taken the loss, which by definition will occur if you start too high, you will be faced with the decision of whether to recover the loss or not with a rollover position. Like the initial position, there is no guarantee that the rollover position will generate a profit.

C. DON'T BUNCH YOUR TRADES NEAR THE UPPER LEVEL OF TRADING

A quick way to big trouble is to bunch your purchases near the upper trading level by using a narrow interval. This unwise

TABLE 8-1

Interval Table for a Debacle
(Upper Trading Level, 400; Interval, 2 Points)

Purchase at	Offset at	Profit Target
398	400	2
396	398	2
394	396	2
392	394	2
390	392	2
388	390	2
386	388	2
384	386	2
382	384	2
380	382	2
		Potential profit = 20 points

practice can be coupled with an additional error of not taking all main-interval positions as the market descends and thus missing all the oscillation profits near the bottom.

Consider the following scenario, which can lead to nightmares.

Wheat prices are at 400. They can't go any lower than 390 and certainly never below 380. Therefore, I will Interval Trade wheat with a small interval, 2 points, so that I can get all of the minor oscillations. I will take contracts down to 380. In the unlikely event that prices temporarily drop below 380, I'll just hold my positions until a rally brings prices above 380.

To see what a debacle this could turn out to be, let's assume the price drops to 300. The 2-point Interval-Trading table for the purchases is given in Table 8–1 and the drawdown table in Table 8–2.

As you can see in these tables, at a price of 380, you would have accumulated 10 contracts. By the time the price is at 300, the drawdown would be $44,500 (each point is worth $50). Your total capital needs would be $51,250 ($6,750 in margin and $44,500 in drawdown). That is a lot of money to put on the line for a potential profit of $1,000. It will take a lot of oscillation profits to make up the difference. Should the market drop another 50 or 100 points, the situation could become most unpleasant.

TABLE 8-2

Drawdown Table for a Debacle

	398	396	394	392	390	388	386	384	382	380	Sum	x$50
380	18	16	14	12	10	8	6	4	2	—	90	$4,500
350	48	46	44	42	40	38	36	34	32	30	390	$19,500
300	98	96	94	92	90	88	86	84	82	80	890	$44,500

D. DON'T USE TOO SMALL OF AN INTERVAL

Suppose in the last scenario you were stubborn and purchased a contract at every 2-point drop from 400 to 300. This would be a 100-point move, a move that is not uncommon for soybeans or wheat. During the drop, you would have purchased 50 contracts. At a price of 300, your drawdown would be $156,250 and your total capital requirements $186,000. Your potential profit would be 100 points or $5,000 (excluding any oscillation profits). The potential rate of return would be 3.2 percent, which is not worth the risk.

Contrast the above figures with those using a 20-point interval. At 300, you would have 5 contracts in inventory and a drawdown of $10,000. Your total capital needs would be $13,375. Your potential profit (excluding oscillation profits) is still $5,000. The potential rate of return is 37 percent, which is worth the risk.

The morals to these calculations are

1. Don't bunch your purchases near the upper trading level.
2. Keep your intervals large.

This is the same advice should you get stuck in a market that goes straight down. Suppose you start Interval Trading a market and, after your first purchase, the market takes off—straight down! Suppose it drops 100 points or more in a matter of a week or two. First of all, realize there will be a bottom down there—somewhere! If your interval is large, and if you have calculated your potential drawdown correctly, and if you are not trading with insufficient funds, it will work out. It might take some time, but chances are it will work. There is no way you could foresee or avoid this situation. You just have to prepare for it.

E. IMPRUDENT ROLLOVERS

It is tempting to say, "I'll always get back my loss by rolling over into a more distant contract." Unfortunately, there is no guarantee that this is true. It might be true; then again, it might not. The rollover problems that can cost you money are

1. A continuing decline.
2. The market turning flat after a decline and remaining that way for an extended period of time, like years.

The Decline Is Not Over

You can't predict the extent of a decline. Therefore, if you use an immediate rollover—a rollover in which you purchase new contracts in the distant month at the same time you offset your expiring contracts—you could compound your problem. You will have all of your losers grouped together at a single rollover price, and, if the decline is not over, the drawdown could be considerably larger than it was before rolling them over. After the rollover, the situation will be the same as if you had bunched all of your purchases near the upper trading level.

For example, suppose you Interval Traded from 400 to 300 using a 20-point interval. At the price of 300, you have accumulated five contracts and a drawdown of $10,000. Let's assume that at 300 you roll the contracts into a distant month at 300. After you roll over, the market collapses to 200. We will take a 100 loss in each of the 5 contracts owned at 300, a total of 500 points. At $50 per point, this is $25,000. Thus the drawdown for the rollover positions is 2.5 times the amount of the original interval.

Rolling contracts into a more distant month may not be the best thing to do. Your loss won't go away by the rollover, and you can set yourself up for an even greater loss. Be reasonably sure the market has passed a major bottom before rolling into a distant month.

Rolling into a Flat Market

One would think that rolling into a flat market would give you a neutral position, one in which you would neither make nor lose money. This is not true. If you roll into a flat market, you will probably lose money.

The reasons for this are buried in the relationship of cash to futures prices. The cash price is the current price of the physical commodity. A futures price is the price that will be paid for the commodity during the delivery month. During the delivery month, the cash price and the futures price for that month merge and become the same value on the last trading day for the futures contract.

A flat market means that the price for the cash commodity remains unchanged for a period of time. The futures price is for the future and has a carrying charge built into its price structure. A carrying charge is the cost of storing a commodity from one delivery month to another. The carrying charges consist of the cost of storage itself, interest, insurance, etc.

Consider the following example. Assume that in September you purchased a December wheat contract for 312 and the cash price at that time was 303 1/2. If the cash market remains flat at 303 1/2, then the price of the December futures contract must drop to that level by December. This will be a decrease of 8 1/2 cents.

Let's assume you roll over 5 contracts (25,000 bushels) of September wheat into the December contract. If the cash market remains flat, you will lose 8 1/2 points per contract or a total of 42 1/2 points ($2,125). In a flat market, an Interval-Trade rollover will lose the amount of the carrying charge no matter what you do. This is built into the mechanics of how the market works.

You can't predict when a market is going to turn flat. Fortunately, flat markets are not common. Even so, they do occur and, if you happen to roll over into one, you will lose money.

As previously mentioned, your best protection is to have reason to believe a major bottom has been put in place before rolling over.

In summary, Interval Trading is not guaranteed to make money. However, if you know what you are doing, diversify your positions, and trade with adequate capital, you should be very successful.

CHAPTER 9

Brokers, Pool Operators, Trading Advisors, and Money Management

Commodity trading is a specialized investment vehicle. Not surprisingly, there are brokers and brokerage firms that specialize in commodity trading. Two other groups that assist the public in commodity trading are commodity pool operators and commodity trading advisors. All of these groups, as well as the individuals within them who deal with the public, must be registered with the Commodity Futures Trading Commission (CFTC), the governmental regulatory agency that regulates futures trading in the United States.

In addition to the CFTC, the futures industry supports their own regulatory association, the National Futures Association (NFA). Membership in the NFA is required for all individuals and groups that provide futures services to the public. To join the NFA, an individual must pass the Series 3 National Commodity Futures Exam.

This chapter provides a brief introduction to commodity brokers, commodity pool operators, commodity trading advisors, and money management.

A. COMMODITY BROKERS

To trade commodities, you must work through a broker. If you wish to trade commodities by Interval Trading, your broker will have to understand how Interval Trading works. If he or she does not, confusion, misunderstanding, and frustration will result.

From the broker's standpoint, Interval Trading requires a special effort to service your account. To Interval Trade correctly, your most recent sale must be used as the offset for your most recent long purchase (last in, first out). This is not how brokerage firm computers are programmed. Their computers will automatically use your most recent sale to offset your oldest long (first in, first out). To prevent this from occurring, you broker will have to override the computer and make the offset entry by hand. Because of ignorance or laziness, some brokers refuse to do this.

If the offsets are not made in the order described in this book (last in, first out), your records and your entire trading scheme will be in total disarray. Problems with offsets could well defeat all of your attempts to make money by Interval Trading.

In choosing your broker, be sure he or she understands Interval Trading. Be sure he or she is willing to offset your trades according to the Interval-Trading technique and not just rely on their computer to do the job for them.

Stockbrokers as Commodity Brokers

If you are new to commodity speculation, it would be logical for you to approach your current stockbroker for advice. You may find, however, that your stockbroker is reluctant or unwilling to take your order for a commodity transaction. There are several reasons for this reluctance. First, his or her office manager may perceive that the potential for an error, which would require compensation to the customer, outweighs the potential for commission revenue. Therefore, the manager may prohibit commodity transactions in his or her branch. Another reason may be that your stockbroker feels uncomfortable with commodity trading and fears that he or she may misadvise you. A retail stockbroker may have considerable expertise in stocks, bonds, mutual funds, annuities, and financial planning but little expertise in commodity speculation.

Some stockbrokers do handle commodity business as an accommodation to their clients even though they may not be well versed in the field. To aid these individuals, many large Wall Street firms designate a person to be a commodity or futures specialist. Your order would probably be relayed to this individual for execution. If you wish to trade commodities, you will be well advised to deal directly with a commodity broker, one who is a specialist in the field.

Commodity Discount Houses

If you are the type of investor who "calls your own shots," you may have an account with a discount firm. Most discount firms that deal in securities do not deal in commodities. However, there are many discount firms that deal exclusively in commodities. Most of these will not handle the contingent orders or offset the trades as required in the Interval-Trading technique outlined in this book. They are volume dealers and cannot be bothered with special requests.

In choosing a broker, another consideration is the net capital requirements maintained by the brokerage firm. Many discount brokers maintain only the mandated minimums. Should a market become very volatile, as lumber did in 1993 or as coffee in 1994, you could be liquidated or find your account transferred to another exchange member not of your choosing.

Introducing Broker (IB)

Another type of commodity broker is the introducing broker. Like the full–service retail broker of a brokerage firm, the introducing broker generates income through commissions on trades. Unlike the full-service retail broker, the introducing broker is not an employee of a commodity brokerage firm (called a futures commission merchant or FCM). Instead, the introducing broker is an independent businessperson who "introduces" his or her accounts to a FCM, who actually places the orders.

An introducing broker may be independent and able to do business with any FCM, or he or she may be guaranteed by one FCM. However, the law requires that the customer's funds must always be deposited with and held by a FCM rather than by the introducing broker. The FCM, not the introducing broker, is responsible for accounting and money security.

Introducing brokers are common in the futures industry because they are less expensive than an employee of a brokerage firm. The advantage to the customer is that the introducing broker is far more eager to please than are some commission house employees. They are also able to exercise a great deal more freedom and become registered in other areas within the commodity industry. The disadvantage is that the introducing broker must cover all of his or her expenses. The money for these expenses comes from commissions.

B. COMMODITY POOL OPERATOR (CPO)

The second group in the commodity industry is the commodity pool operator or CPO. The role of the CPO is to provide a method for small investors to speculate with limited risk. In general, one who participates in a commodity pool or fund loses control of his or her money. This may be an acceptable trade-off for the limited risk usually offered.

A commodity pool is usually a limited partnership. The investors deposit funds in the partnership, which are then used to trade commodities. It is very important for you to verify that the pool is indeed a limited partnership before sending funds to it. Not all commodity pools are limited partnerships; some are general partnerships. In a general partnership, you will be liable for losses that exceed the amount of initial capitalization.

Another aspect of being involved with a futures fund is the compensation arrangements for the person running the pool who in most cases, is the general partner. Sometimes the fees and organizational expenses charged to the fund are so enormous that pools must make a tremendous rate of return if anything is going to be returned to the investor.

Often there is a minimum amount of time you must leave your investment in a commodity pool (usually six months). In addition, you may not be able to withdraw your funds at will. Some pools allow you to withdraw your funds only upon written notice once a quarter.

C. COMMODITY TRADING ADVISOR (CTA)

A separate and distinct entity from a commodity broker and commodity pool operator is the commodity trading advisor or CTA.

The role of a CTA is to manage a client's account. This is accomplished by actually trading the account or advising the client to take specific trades. The CTA works through a commodity broker but derives his or her income from fees rather than from a commission.

A CTA can be an individual or a company. If the CTA is an individual, then he or she must be a member of the NFA. If the CTA is a company, then all officers must be members of the NFA.

A CTA is the commodity industry equivalent of a registered investment advisor or RIA in the securities field. RIAs manage stock and bond portfolios for individuals as well as for corporations, pension funds, and mutual funds. CTAs perform a similar function in the futures industry, but there are some important differences. Like an RIA, the CTA is paid fees rather than commissions. Unlike an RIA, it is legal for a CTA to have a portion of the fees based on incentive—that is, a CTA can share in the profits that are generated in a customer's account. Some CTAs charge a flat fixed management fee while others charge only an incentive fee. Most, however, charge some combination of both management and incentive fees.

For many people, using a CTA is the best way to speculate in commodities. Successful futures trading, unlike investing in stocks and bonds, consumes a great deal of time. Many people do not have the time, temperament, and talent for trading commodities. A CTA that uses a sensible and systematic trading approach, like the one detailed in this book, can be an important addition to an individual or corporate portfolio. Today, investing in managed futures has emerged as a separate asset class since the pioneering work was done by the late Dr. John Linter of Harvard University in the early 1980s. Portfolio managers of the 1990s now look at how much of their portfolios to allocate to equities (stocks), fixed income (bonds), cash (Treasuries and money funds), and managed futures.

D. MANAGED MONEY AND PORTFOLIO DIVERSIFICATION

Why should someone consider becoming involved with an investment area as speculative as commodities futures trading? The answer might surprise you. Look at Figure 9–1. This figure shows the power of investment diversification. The left side of the figure illustrates the growth of $100,000 over a 25-year period at a continuous 6 percent rate of return. This type of an investment would be made by a person who has safety of principal foremost in mind. This investor would probably put his or her money in fixed-income investments with short maturities and probably want government guarantees as well. Typical investments would be Treasury bills (T-bills), insured certificates of deposit (CDs), and FDIC insured savings or interest-bearing checking accounts.

Now look at the right side of that same figure. Notice how the same $100,000 could have been invested for the same 25 years. But look how spreading out the investment risks not only can make for substantially higher overall returns, but can actually reduce the risk of low returns or even negative returns. This example shows a loss of 20 percent of the initial sum (that's a $20,000 loss of principal at the start of the investment program) and no return on another 20 percent over the entire 25 years. Another $20,000 is assumed to provide only a 5 percent rate of return (less than the cautious investor did on the entire sum for 25 years). But look at the effect of a 10 percent return on $20,000 for 25 years and 15 percent on the remaining $20,000. It is staggering! This illustrates the power of diversification in an overall investment portfolio.

Now look at Figure 9–2, the classical investment pyramid, to see some possible investments for our diversified portfolio. At the base of the pyramid are those investments that have safety and liquidity. These investments include savings accounts, insured CDs, money market funds, interest-bearing checking accounts, equity in your home, cash value in your life insurance, fixed annuities, T-bills, and plain old cash. The next higher level represents a variety of investments that you might own for income and long–term growth. These include high–grade corporate or (depending on your tax bracket) municipal bonds, investment grade ("blue chip") common stocks, utility company stocks, preferred stocks, investment real estate, and variable annuities. T-notes and T-bonds would fall into this category, not because of any credit risk on the

FIGURE 9-1

The Power of Diversification as an Investment Strategy

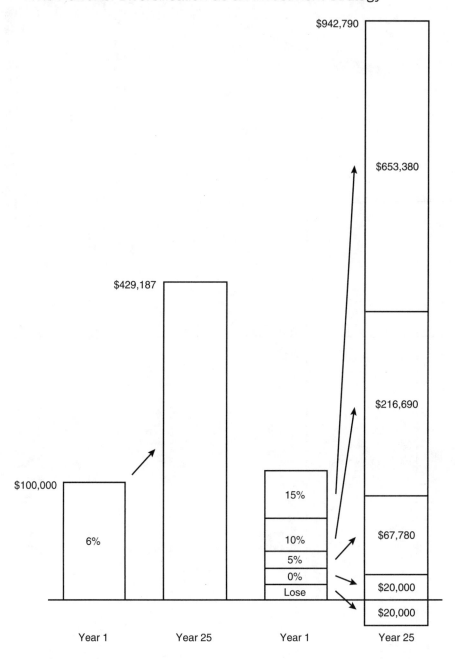

FIGURE 9-2

The Investment Pyramid

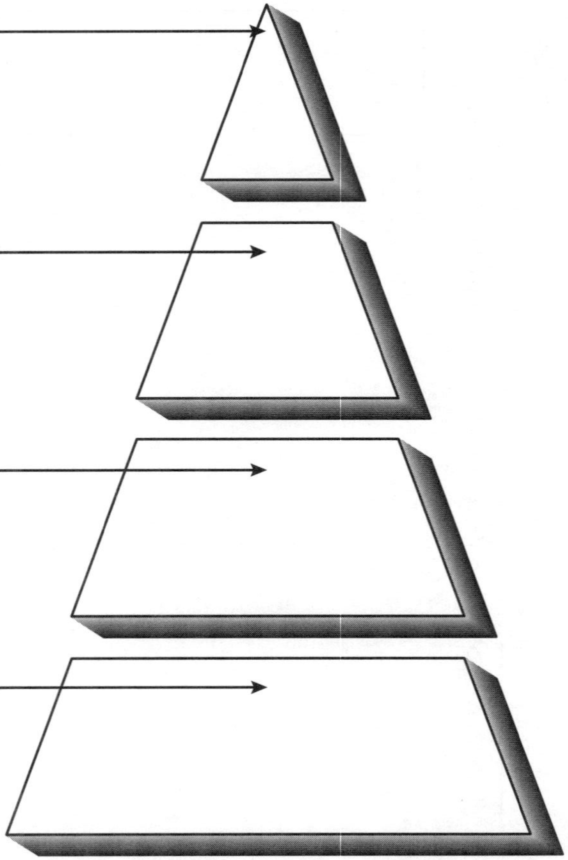

High Risk

- Raw land
- Tax shelters
- Penny stocks

- Commodities on your own
- Short selling stocks or options
- Collectibles

Speculation and Aggressive Growth

- Speculative common stock
- Managed futures

- Lower-quality and or deeply discounted corporate bonds/municipal bonds
- Option buying

Income and Long-Term Growth

- Investment real estate
- High-grade municipal/ corporate bonds
- Utility common stocks

- Investment grade and good quality stocks
- Variable annuities
- Preferred stock
- U.S. Treasury notes and bonds

Liquidity and Safety

- Passbook savings
- CD's
- Life insurance
- Money market funds

- U.S. Treasury bills
- Fixed annuities
- Equity in a home
- Interest bearing checking
- Cash

part of the issuer (the U.S. government) but because they are longer in maturity than T-bills and, therefore, subject to market risk should interest rates change.

The next higher level in the investment pyramid contains aggressive growth investments, such as speculative common stocks, lower–quality or deeply discounted bonds, option buying programs, and managed futures accounts.

The very top of the pyramid are investments for those people who are fortunate enough to have true speculative risk capital. Investments at the top include trading futures on your own, selling stocks and options short, investing in raw land, investing in collectibles (mostly due to their illiquidity), buying "penny stocks," and investing in the few remaining tax shelters.

The important thing to remember about the investment pyramid is that investments become potentially more profitable but also more risky the farther up the pyramid you go. Investments toward the base of the pyramid will offer a lower rate of return but will also be safer than those toward the top of the pyramid.

Let's go back to the right side of Figure 9–1. Let's say 20 percent of the $100,000 that was lost was squandered in tax shelters, short selling options, and attempting to trade commodities on your own. This, unfortunately, is a very realistic scenario. Now let's say the $20,000 that produced no return during the 25–year period was invested in high-risk common stocks (some of which "hit" and others did not) as well as investment surprises (low–risk investments that for whatever reason failed to live up to their expectations). The $20,000 that produced a 5 percent return were those investments placed in CDs and short maturity T-bills. The $20,000 which made a 10 percent return may well have been invested in "blue chip" stocks and investment–grade bonds. Very likely, the $20,000 that produced the 15 percent return was invested in managed futures or a high-risk managed securities product like an aggressive growth mutual fund or a combination of the two. This is the answer that might surprise you. To arrive at a blended rate of return that will substantially exceed the 6 percent savings rate, you must take some risks! To outperform inflation you must take some risks. A well–managed futures investment can go a very long way toward accomplishing this goal.

One final word about getting involved in futures trading: *Be Careful*. There are unfortunately a lot of very convincing telephone solicitors in the commodity business. They often move from place to place selling unproved performance to an unsuspecting public. Most of the "investment opportunities" they push fail completely. Never send money to anyone until you have checked them out carefully. More people suffer needless financial damage in the commodity industry than probably any other industry except gaming.

CHAPTER 10

Examples of Interval-Traded Markets

This chapter contains five examples of Interval-Traded markets, one example from each of the diversification groups presented in Chapter 11. Each market was Interval Traded from 3/1/94 to the middle of November (or December in the case of January orange juice). By choosing this time period, the results from all of the contracts can be compared using the same time period, and the outcome of the rollover of the December 1994 live hog contract into 1995 could be included.

Each market was chosen with hindsight to illustrate a feature of Interval Trading. The examples are not intended to represent real-time trading, although each example could have been traded as shown. The paper trading assumed that if the market merely touched a price, the fill would have been made at that price. This is not realistic. In real life, some slippage would have occurred. Therefore, the results would be lower than presented.

The examples are presented in order of increasing problems associated with the contract. Each example will be discussed separately. The five contracts used for examples are:

Orange juice, January 1995
Wheat, December 1994
Crude oil, December 1994
Gold (COMEX), December 1994
Live hogs, December 1994

TABLE 10-1

Summary of Results without Rollover

Commodity	Number of Trades	Gross Profit <loss>
Orange juice	17	$12,202
Wheat	5	3,125
Crude oil	5	3,720
Gold	5	3,740
Live hogs	3	<7,830>
Total	35	$14,957
Less commissions at $50 per roundturn		1,750
Net		$13,207

A. SUMMARY OF RESULTS

The results of Interval Trading with no attempt to recover the losses by rollovers is summarized in Table 10–1. As you can see, four of the five markets were profitable. The fifth, December live hogs, was a big loser.

Although maximum drawdown in each of the five markets did not occur at the same time, drawdown was significant during the months of August and September. The maximum drawdown of each contract is as follows:

Orange juice	9/9/94	$14,100
Wheat	7/7/94	850
Crude oil	8/22/94	3,200
Gold	8/4/94	950
Live hogs	11/15/94	7,930
	Total	$26,930

We can use this maximum drawdown figure to determine the size of an account needed to Interval Trade these five contracts. You would need at least $50,000, approximately twice the size of the drawdown. A larger account would provide a larger safety factor.

With a $50,000 account, the rate of return without any rollover would have been

$$(13,207/50,000) \times 100 = 26\%$$

T A B L E 10–2

Summary of Results with Rollover

Commodity	Number of Trades	Gross Profit <loss>
Orange juice	17	$12,202
Wheat	5	3,125
Crude oil	5	3,720
Gold	5	3,740
Live hogs	9	0
Total	41	$22,787
Less commissions at $50 per roundturn		2,050
Net		$20,737

Had you rolled over the live hogs, you would have recovered your lost capital, but as of October 1995, not any of the hoped for profit. The results for the rollover, are given in Table 10–2. Your rate of return on a $50,000 account using this strategy would have been

$$(20,737/50,000) \times 100 = 41\%$$

B. ORANGE JUICE

The 1995 January orange juice contract is the perfect example of successful Interval Trading. When trading commenced on 3/1/94, the orange juice market was in a downtrend. The bottom occurred at a price of 89 in September. The resulting uptrend was strong enough that all open contracts were offset before the closing date of 12/20/95. No rollovers were needed. The market provided considerable oscillation profits during the trading period.

This is an example of a very successful market that did have a hefty drawdown. At its bottom (89), a total of five contracts were held and the drawdown was over $14,000. To be successful in Interval Trading, you must have both an account large enough to handle this type of drawdown without stress and a personality that can withstand this type of financial pressure.

TABLE 10-3

January Orange Juice 10-Year High–Low Prices

Year	High	Low
1985	185.60	108.50
1986	180.00	92.90
1987	131.50	83.60
1988	180.50	111.80
1989	178.50	130.85
1990	201.00	121.00
1991	196.75	99.00
1992	178.80	112.65
1993	163.00	77.50
1994	133.70	82.15

The Upper Trading Level and Interval-Trading Table

Table 10–3 contains the high–low prices for January orange juice from 1985 through 1994. These values were used to calculate the upper trading level and first purchase price for the January 1995 contract.

The extreme values were a high of 201 (1990) and a low of 77.50 (1993). These values are used to calculate the one-third level as follows:

High:	201.00
Low:	77.50
Difference:	123.50
Divide by 3:	41.16
Add to low:	118 (truncated)

The one-third value gives us our first purchase at 118. For orange juice, an interval of 10 was used (see Table 5–4).

The upper trading level is calculated by adding the interval to the first purchase price. For January 1995 orange juice, the value was (10 + 118) = 128. These values were used to construct the Interval-Trading table, Table 10–4.

TABLE 10-4

Interval-Trading Table for 1995 January Orange Juice
(Upper Trading Level, 128; Interval, 10)

Main Buy	Sell-Buy	Offset	Profit
—	123	128	5
118	—	123	5
—	113	118	5
108	—	113	5
—	103	108	5
98	—	103	5
—	93	98	5
88	—	93	5

Summary of Results

Trading results for January 1995 orange juice are summarized in
Table 10–5 and Figure 10–1. As you can see, a profit of $12,202
was realized on 17 trades from 3/1/94 through 12/20/94. Five contracts were held at the low of 89 on 9/9/94 for a total drawdown of
about $14,000.

C. WHEAT

Wheat illustrates two problems in Interval Trading—(1) the possibility of two or more one-third-levels (and thus upper trading
levels) and (2) a market that moves above the upper trading level
in a major bull move.

The Upper Trading Level and Interval-Trading Table

Table 10–6 contains the high–low prices for December wheat from
1984 through 1993. Inspection of the table shows a high value of
440 occurring in 1989 and again in 1992.

The low value need for the calculation is a little more difficult
to select. The absolute low for the 10-year period is 238, occurring

T A B L E 10-5

Summary of Trades for 1995 January Orange Juice

Purchases		Offsets		Profit <loss>
3/1/94	117.00*	12/20/94	117.60†	0.60
4/4/94	108.00	4/7/94	113.00	5.00
4/7/94	113.00	11/17/94	118.25‡	5.25
4/15/94	108.00	4/28/94	113.00	5.00
5/4/94	108.00	10/20/94	113.00	5.00
5/10/94	98.00	5/25/94	103.00	5.00
5/25/94	103.00	10/17/94	108.00	5.00
6/16/94	98.00	7/20/94	103.00	5.00
7/21/94	98.00	7/29/94	103.00	5.00
8/29/94	98.00	9/26/94	103.00	5.00
9/30/94	98.00	10/14/94	103.50‡	5.50
10/24/94	108.00	11/3/94	113.00	5.00
11/21/94#	112.00	12/19/94	118.00	5.00
11/21/94#	108.00	12/6/94	113.00	5.00
11/22/94	103.00	11/28/94	108.00	5.00
11/30/94	103.00	12/6/94	108.00	5.00
12/12/94	108.00	12/14/94	113.00	5.00
			Total	81.35 ($12,202)

*Close on 3/1/94 was below the main buy level of 108.
†Trade on close 12/20/94.
‡Open was above the target sell level.
#Both trades would have occurred on the same day: Open, 112.00; High, 113.50; Low, 107.55; close, 107.55

T A B L E 10-6

December Wheat 10-Year High–Low Prices

	Year	High	Low
	1984	418	337
	1985	364	279
	1986	309	244
	1987	325	247
	1988	438	289
	1989	440	378
	1990	380	238
	1991	407	272
	1992	440	312
	1993	373	294

FIGURE 10–1

1995 January Orange Juice

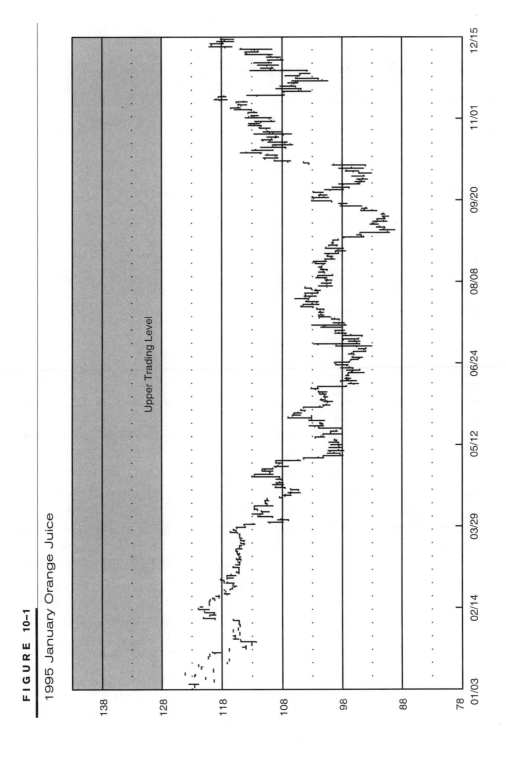

TABLE 10–7

Interval-Trading Table for 1994 December Wheat
(Upper Trading Level, 353; Interval, 25 Cents)

Main Buy	Sell-Buy	Offset	Profit
—	340.5	353	12.5
328	—	340.5	12.5
—	315.5	328	12.5
303	—	315.5	12.5

in 1990. The next most recent low is 272, which occurred in 1991. Using both of these low values, we can calculate two possible one-third values.

High:	440	440
Low:	238	272
Difference:	202	168
Divide by 3:	67	56
Add to low:	305	328

These two values provide two possible choices for a first-position entry value, 305 and 328. They differ by about one interval (25 points). Which one should you use? It's a guess. If you chose the lower value, you would not have Interval Traded December wheat in 1994. The price never went lower than 324 (See Figure 10–2). However, if you had chosen the higher value, you would have Interval Traded the contract. Using a 25-point interval and the 328 value, the upper trading level would have been set at 353. The interval table is given in Table 10–7.

How do you choose between two or more one-third levels? There is no foolproof method. If you choose the one that is too high, you could have excessive drawdown as well as rollover problems. If you choose the one that is too low, you may not trade at all. Is 328 too high? It gives an upper trading level of 353, which has been exceeded in 8 of the last 10 years and all 6 of the last 6 years. From that standpoint, it is not unreasonable.

TABLE 10-8

Summary of Trades for 1994 December Wheat

Purchases		Offsets		Profit <loss>
4/14/94	328	4/29/94	340.5	12.5
4/29/94	340.5	5/23/94	353	12.5
5/26/94	340.5	6/7/94	353	12.5
6/20/94	340.5	8/11/94	353	12.5
7/5/94	328	7/18/94	340.5	12.5
			Total	62.5 ($3125)

In choosing high and low values for the one-third calculation, you have to use common sense. There is no one formula that will work in all markets all of the time. Inspect the 10-year highs and lows, or use a monthly or weekly chart if you wish. Select reasonable values and use them for your calculation.

Summary of Results

Interval Trading December 1994 wheat would have been both profitable and frustrating. The market finished very strong. A major portion of the bull phase would have been missed by pure Interval Trading since it occurred above the upper trading level. This market illustrates the case of a strong market where switching from Interval Trading to a trend-following method would have been the correct course of action. With hindsight, you can see exactly where the switch should have occurred. However, in the real world, the correct time to switch would not have been apparent.

Table 10-8 summarizes the trades that would have been made using the Interval-Trading table given in Table 10-7. As you can see, no losses were sustained. Figure 10-2 is a chart of the daily prices covering the trading period.

D. CRUDE OIL

The Upper Trading Level and Interval-Trading Table

The high-low values from 1984 through 1993 for December crude oil are given in Table 10-9.

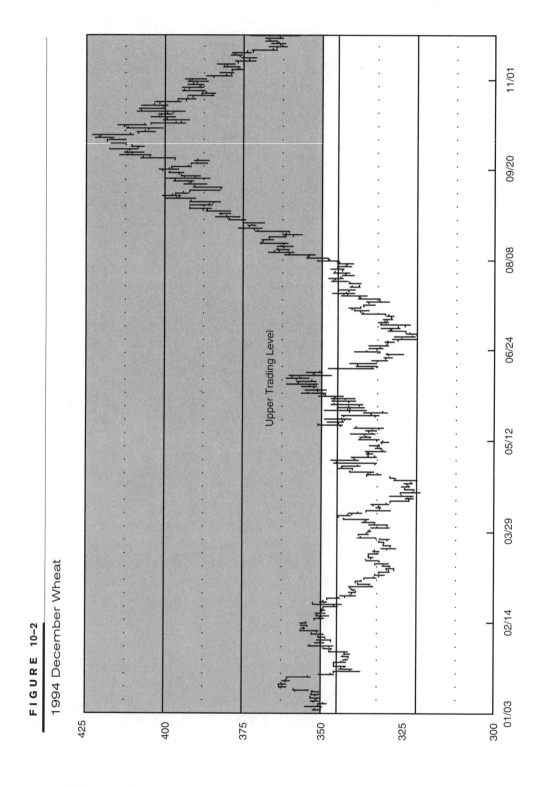

FIGURE 10-2

1994 December Wheat

Upper Trading Level

TABLE 10–9

December Crude Oil 10-Year High–Low Prices

Year	High	Low
1984	31.60	26.93
1985	31.82	23.90
1986	26.45	10.40
1987	21.65	16.40
1988	18.35	12.13
1989	20.67	12.70
1990	39.90	17.65
1991	27.98	17.10
1992	24.00	17.89
1993	23.00	16.35

TABLE 10–10

Interval-Trading Table for 1994 December Crude Oil
(Upper Trading Level, 22; Interval, 2)

Main Buy	Sell-Buy	Offset	Profit
—	21	22	1
20	—	21	1
—	19	20	1
18	—	19	1
—	17	18	1
16	—	17	1
—	15	16	1
14	—	15	1

The absolute high, 39.90, occurred in 1990 just prior to the Persian Gulf War. The absolute low, 10.40, occurred in 1986. Using these two extreme values, the one-third level is calculated to be 20.23. Interestingly, similar values are obtained using the 1991 high and the 1992 low as well as the 1991 high and the 1993 low. With a one-third level of 20 and an interval of 2, the upper trading level becomes 22. The interval table is given in Table 10–10.

T A B L E 10-11

Summary of Trades for 1994 December Crude Oil

Purchases		Offsets		Profit <loss>
3/1/94	16.00	5/6/94	17.00	1
5/6/94	17.00	6/15/94	18.00	1
6/15/94	18.00	7/12/94	19.00	1
7/12/94	19.00	11/4/94	18.72	<0.28>
8/12/94	18.00	11/3/94	19.00	1
			Total	3.72 ($3720)

Summary of Results

Table 10–11 summarizes the trades that would have been taken using the Interval-Trading table given in Table 10–10. Figure 10–3 is a chart of the daily prices covering the trading period.

December 1994 crude oil is an example of a market that moved sideways during the trading period. The market did not close above the upper trading level, nor did it end on a firm tone. Consequently, one of the trades resulted in a loss. The loss was small ($280) and less than one-half interval. No attempt should have been made to recover it with a rollover.

E. GOLD

The Upper Trading Level and Interval-Trading Table

The high–low prices for December gold from 1984 through 1993 are given in Table 10–12.

To illustrate another method for the selection of the high and low for calculation, let's use the 10-year averages of the highs (492.30) and lows (342.70).

High	492.30
Low	342.70
Difference	149.60
Divide by 3	48.90
Add to low	392 (rounded up)

FIGURE 10-3

1994 December Crude Oil

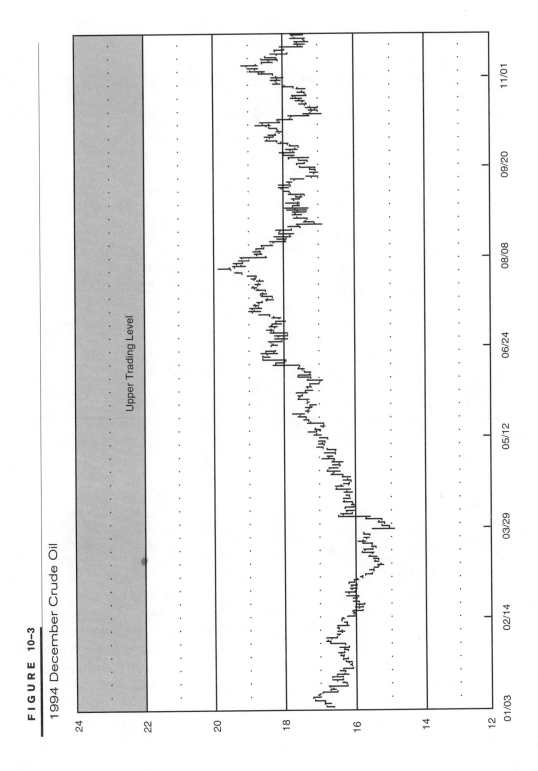

T A B L E 10–12

December Gold 10-Year High–Low Prices

Year	High	Low
1984	608.00	304.70
1985	489.50	301.50
1986	446.50	336.50
1987	502.30	365.00
1988	546.00	395.50
1989	516.00	360.60
1990	457.40	357.00
1991	484.20	346.00
1992	442.70	328.90
1993	429.80	331.70

T A B L E 10–13

Interval-Trading Table for 1994 December Gold
(Upper Trading Level, 400; Interval, 20)

Main Buy	Sell-Buy	Offset	Profit
—	390	400	10
380	—	390	10
—	370	380	10
360	—	370	10

With an interval of 10, the upper trading level would be 412 and the one-half interval just below it, 402. This brings up another point in considering the upper trading level. Commodity prices often stop at round numbers like 400. Therefore, it is not a good idea to have your offsets and purchases just above a major round number like 400. In fact, it is a very bad idea to have your upper trading level one-half interval above a major round number like 400. Therefore, let's adjust the upper trading level to 400, use a 20-point interval, and construct an interval table using these figures. (See Table 10–13.)

T A B L E   10–14

Summary of Trades for 1994 December Gold

Purchases		Offsets		Profit <loss>
4/22/94	380.00	5/6/94	390.00	10
5/6/94	390.00	5/23/94	400.40	10
6/1/94	390.00	6/17/94	400.00	10
7/6/94	390.00	9/23/94	400.00	10
10/11/94	390.00	11/15/94	387.40	<2.60>
				Total 37.40 ($3740)

Summary of Results

Table 10–14 summarizes the trades made in the December 1994 gold contract and Figure 10–4 is a daily chart covering the trading period.

The December 1994 gold contract traded sideways during the period and ended in a downtrend. This market illustrates the ability of Interval Trading to take profits from a sideways market where a trend-following method would have failed.

Because the market ended in a downtrend, a loss had to be taken in one of the contracts. The loss was small so no rollover should have been considered.

F. LIVE HOGS

The Upper Trading Level and Interval-Trading Table

The high–low prices for December live hogs from 1984 through 1993 is given in Table 10–15.

As you can see from Figure 10–5, it really didn't make much difference where we set our upper trading level for the December 1994 hog contract. The market went almost straight down with no rallies, well below the absolute 10-year low. Therefore, let's use the 10-year averages for the calculations and see the effect of the larger interval on drawdown and the results of rollover into 1995.

F I G U R E   10-4

1994 December Gold

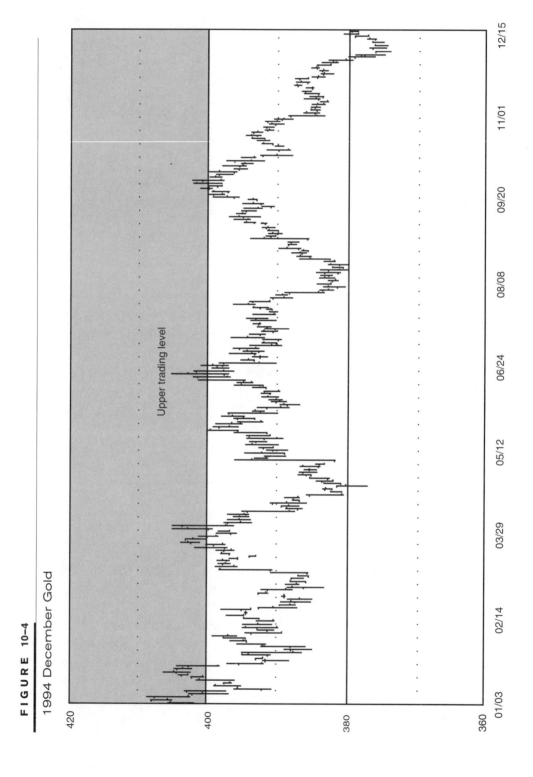

TABLE 10–15

December Live Hogs 10-Year High–Low Prices

Year	High	Low
1984	58.40	45.42
1985	50.40	36.35
1986	57.60	38.37
1987	49.85	38.05
1988	48.05	38.30
1989	53.67	40.55
1990	56.10	44.25
1991	48.92	40.12
1992	45.15	39.10
1993	51.50	40.07

TABLE 10–16

Interval-Trading Table for 1994 December Live Hogs
(Upper Trading Level, 48; Interval, 4)

Main Buy	Sell-Buy	Offset	Profit
—	46	48	2
44	—	46	2
—	42	44	2
40	—	42	2
—	38	40	2
36	—	38	2
—	34	36	2
32	—	34	2

The average high for the last 10 years was 51.96, and the average low was 40.06. These values give a one-third level of 44 (truncated). With an interval of 4 (400 points), the upper trading level would be 48. The interval table constructed using these values is given in Table 10–16.

TABLE 10-17

Summary of Trades for 1994 December Live Hogs

Purchases		Offsets		Profit <loss>
4/28/94	44.00	11/15/94	33.475	<10.525>
7/5/94	40.00	11/15/94	33.475	<6.525>
10/4/94	36.00	11/15/94	33.475	<2.525>
			Total	<19.575> (<$7830>)

Summary of Results

Table 10–17 summarizes the trades made in the December 1994 live hog contract and Figure 10–5 is a daily chart covering the trading period.

Trading in the December 1994 live hog contract began, like that in the January 1995 orange juice, with prices in a major downtrend. The difference in the two contracts is that the orange juice recovered partway through the trading period to provide a handsome profit while the hogs did not. This hog contract was chosen to illustrate what to do when a major loss is sustained at the end of the contract's life.

Rollovers

The total loss in the December 1994 live hog contract was 19.57. Three contracts were involved. Therefore, our average loss was 6.52 per contract. Our rollover strategy will be an immediate rollover of three contracts on termination of the December contract with an initial profit objective of 6.525 per contract to recover our capital.

We offset our December contracts on 11/15/94 and purchased three July 1995 contracts on the close of that day at 42.725. Our target price would be:

Without hoped-for profit: 42.72 + 6.52 = 49.24

FIGURE 10-5

1994 December Live Hogs

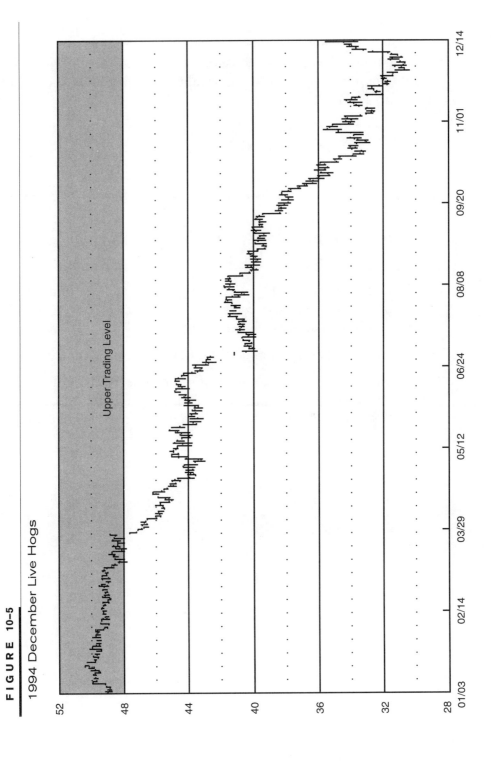

The July contract never reached our target price. Had we been astute, we would have offset at 48. Chances are, however, we would not have been astute and would have hung on to the end of the contract on 6/15/95.

Gain on the July contract:

6/15/95 close:	45.72
11/15/94 close:	42.72
Profit per contract:	3.00
Gross on 3 contracts:	9.00

The remaining amount needed for recovery was:

$6.52 - 3.00 = 3.52$ per contract for 3 contracts.

The rollover was continued into the October 1995 contract by the purchase of three contracts on the close of 6/15/95 at 42.07. Our new target price per contract was:

October contract target price: $42.075 + 3.525 = 45.600$

Our target price was exceeded on 8/21/95, completing a rollover without profit. Daily charts of the July 1995 and the October 1995 live hog contracts are given in Figures 10–6 and 10–7.

1995 July Live Hogs

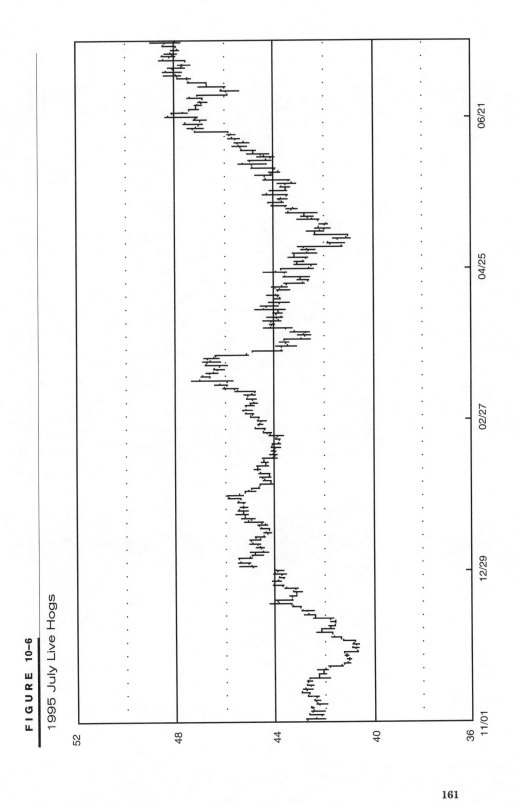

FIGURE 10-7

1995 October Live Hogs

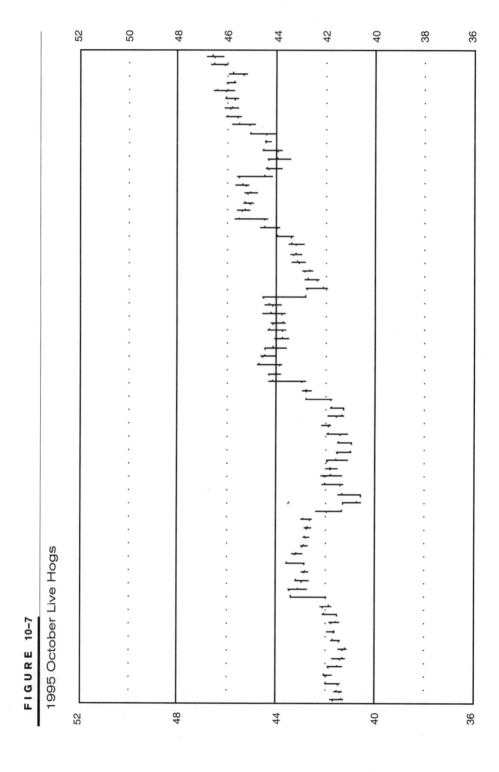

CHAPTER 11

Intelligent Commodity Speculation

The goal of intelligent commodity speculation is to obtain a high return on our capital at the lowest possible risk. To attain this goal, we trade most commodities using the Interval Trading method.

The basic elements of intelligent commodity speculation are

1. Adequate capital.
2. Diversification.
3. Interval Trading.

A. ADEQUATE CAPITAL

Nothing can be gained by trading commodities with inadequate capital. The possibility of losing money by trading with an under-funded account is very high, even if you are correct in the selection of all variables. The reason is the same reason that makes Interval Trading successful: commodity prices tend to oscillate. When commodity prices are trending, it seems that for every two steps forward, there is one step backward. Commodity prices are also known for making major price runs, both up and down, with no warning and often for no apparent reason. These oscillations and price excursions generally correct themselves, leaving an intact trend or pattern. However, with an underfunded account,

these price aberrations exacerbate drawdown and can force liqui-
dation. With intervals of the proper size and the funds to carry
the inventory, price aberrations can provide oscillation profits.

Prudent money management states that you should never
have more than about one-third of your total speculation capital
committed to margin and drawdown at any one time. If you have
inadequate capital and follow the money management rule, you
will be restricted in your Interval Trading to just one commodity.
Interval Trading only one commodity violates a cardinal rule of
intelligent commodity speculation: *diversify your holdings.* If you
Interval Trade only one commodity, and if you are so unlucky as
to pick the wrong one, you could be stuck for a considerable period
of time with no profits. To avoid this, you must diversify.

What is adequate capital for Interval Trading? You will need
at a minimum $50,000. With $50,000, you will be able to diversify
and trade at least three different commodities. Obviously, more
capital would be better.

B. DIVERSIFICATION

Although it is possible to identify which commodities are suitable
for Interval Trading, it is impossible to predict which of these
would be the best one. Therefore, to protect ourselves, we must diversify. However, merely trading three different commodities is not
diversification. We must trade commodities that are not related.

Consider the groups of commodities listed in Table 11–1.
These are, for the most part, unrelated groups of commodities. Except for the food and fibers, the commodities within a group tend
to move in tandem. They do not move in a lockstep fashion, as the
contract months within one commodity tend to do. The commodities within the groups all just tend to move in the same general
direction. When the grains are up, they are, in general, all up.
When the metals are down, they are, again in general, all down.
This is not always true, but it is true often enough that when considering diversification we will assume it to be true.

The reason for the general tendency of commodities within a
group to move in the same direction is that they are fundamen-
tally related one way or another. A factor that affects the supply

TABLE 11-1

Commodity Groups for Diversification

Grains and Oilseeds	*Energy Complex*
Wheat	Crude oil
Corn	Unleaded gasoline
Oats	Heating oil
Soybeans	Natural gas
Soybean meal	
Soybean oil	*Food and Fibers*
	Sugar
Livestock and Meat	Coffee
Live hogs	Cotton
Pork bellies	Orange juice
Live cattle	Lumber
Feeder cattle	
Metals	
Gold	
Silver	
Copper	
Platinum	
Palladium	

and demand of one of the group will affect them all in the same general way. A drought in the Midwest, for example, will drive up the grains by limiting their supply. A disagreement within OPEC as to the limitation on the production of crude oil, will drive down the price of crude oil. The prices of other commodities in the energy complex will also fall because they are derived or made from crude oil in some fashion. However, a drought in the Midwest will have little effect on the price of crude oil, and the price of crude oil will have little effect on the price of the grains. In general, the prices of the two commodity groups are unrelated. Granted, the price of oil at the farm can affect the price of grains, but the price of crude oil is not a driving factor behind the price of corn or wheat as it is a driving force affecting the price of heating oil and unleaded gasoline.

The purchase of three contracts of wheat or three contracts of crude oil is not diversification. The purchase of a contract of

wheat, corn, and soybeans is not diversification, nor is the purchase of a contract of crude oil, heating oil, and unleaded gasoline.
However, the purchase of a contract of wheat and a contract of
crude oil is diversification. For that matter, the purchase of any of
the grains and any of the energy complex is diversification.

The concept of diversification is thus very simple. You should
hold as many different types of commodities as possible before
you buy two of any one group. If your capital allows you to purchase only three contracts, then purchase only one from each of
the groups.

As mentioned above, the food and fibers group is an excep-
tion. The commodities in this group are really individual commodities, and each will have little effect upon the other. You can
diversify completely by making all of your purchases within this
group alone.

In order to diversify, one of the commodities within a group
must be suitable for Interval Trading. This means that it must be
close to or in the lower one-third of its last 10-year price range. It
should be at least in the lower one-half of that price range. If all
commodities in a group are in the upper one-half of their 10-year
price range, you should not trade any of them. In this case you
cannot diversify into that group. Interval Trade only those commodities that are suitable. You are better off putting your capital
in T-bills than to Interval Trade commodities that are too high
priced.

C. INTERVAL TRADING

The majority of this book has been devoted to a discussion of the
Interval Trading technique. When large intervals and the sell-buy
strategy are used in Interval Trading, consistent and continuous
profits can be realized. While speculation is speculation and you
should never risk more than you can afford to lose, Interval Trading can provide a high return on your capital with an acceptable
level of risk.

INDEX